Dedication

This book is dedicated to women around the
world who face the abuses written herein.
And for Anne — wherever you are
A promise kept

Foreword

The main character of August Storms is a composite of 16 women I have spoken with who were gracious enough to tell me their life experiences and let me into their hearts and thought processes. They shall remain anonymous. Some were witnesses to abuse or were abused themselves, as children. Some were not abused until after they were with their partner. Nearly all of them exhibited a low self-esteem, however and were poorly educated. Their economic status prevented them from making the decision to move on. They felt that there was nowhere to go. I am sorry for their pain and pray that they can find some way to heal. Their emotional scars are almost as visible and just as devastating as their physical ones. I have drawn from their experiences in writing this book. It is not a figment of my imagination. Intimate Partner Violence (IPV) is real and has long lasting, damaging effects.

Domestic violence has many forms other than physical, including emotional/psychological, sexual, economic deprivation and threats of doing bodily harm. The Office of Violence Against Women (OVW) defines domestic violence as a "pattern of abusive behavior in any relationship that is used by one partner to gain or maintain power and control over another intimate partner." Through my research, I have discovered that nearly all victims of IPV have had to deal with multiple forms of abuse on a daily basis. Domestic violence is a serious, preventable public health problem that affects 32 million Americans. That is 10% of the population. (CDC)

Many advocates and counselors describe domestic violence as a pattern of behaviors. IPV can be progressive throughout the relationship. It can start off by one partner controlling certain aspects of the other partner's life, only to escalate as time goes on. Over time, the abusive spouse has taken control over all finances, the automobile, and access to friends and family, denying the victim resources and leaving them destitute. Also, the victims may be prevented from finishing education or obtaining employment.

It is my hope that this book will bring about awareness of this national problem and prevent the abuses, like those that have occurred to the women I have talked to. It is mainly written for young women ages 15-35, who may be making choices on the type of individual they should choose as a mate. Others may also find the book, if not disturbing, both useful and informative. Men may be victims also, but women are six times more likely to be abused.

My main focus is getting the victim to understand that there are problems and finding acceptable solutions to them. If you happen to be in an abusive relationship, you need to get out of the environment and seek help. Do not accept or tolerate, for any length of time, abuse of any kind. It is highly unlikely that a victim is going to change the abuser. Before it is too late, a difficult decision is going to have to be made. Do you stay with the abuser and accept the maltreatment or call for help and put your trust in complete strangers.

In an abusive situation, most victims, women in particular, feel that there is no place to turn for help. The victim feels trapped and alone. In the past, shelters and law enforcement agencies had been ineffective in preventing abuse and only succeeded in making the abuser more abusive. However, this no longer seems to be the case. As domestic violence has been brought into public view, the response to it has evolved into a well-oiled machine. It is dealt with through the combined efforts of law enforcement agencies, the courts, social service agencies, and corrections/probation agencies.

Domestic violence was once thought of as a private family matter, however this, too, is no longer the case. Activism, initiated by victim advocacy and feminist groups, has led to better understanding of the wide spectrum and effects of domestic violence on victims and families. This has brought about significant changes in both legislation and the response of the criminal justice system. The bottom line: if you feel that you are in an abusive situation, do not try to rationalize it by saying that it will never happen, again. Get out. Leave the next choice up to the abuser. If the individual is serious about keeping you, then that person is going to get professional help. Do not fall for false promises that the abuser makes when he/she says that he/she is going to get help. It is going to take months of intense counseling and possibly drug therapy to control aggression. If you do not seek help, as the victim, one thing is certain. It will likely continue to get worse.

—   Michael A. Pealo

Table of Contents

Acknowledgements

With a first novel, especially on a topic such as this, I needed individuals to support me in the endeavor. I would like to acknowledge their thoughts and concerns which have proved invaluable. Without their assistance and insight, this book could not have been published.

I would first like to thank the publishers at The Pancoast Concern; President Brian Pancoast and Don Kneeland for red-lining and mentoring me through the difficult process. I am grateful for their vast knowledge base; and Duane Pancoast for the cover design and photo.

Thanks to the community for your prayers and encouragement and to the Marion Public Library for technical support.

Special thanks to the following individuals for reading and commenting on early rough drafts. Without your input and ideas, this book would not be what it is today:

Mr. Ernest Rehor, my high school English teacher who also gave me a love for the language; Ms. Lucinda Dey, your insight and kind words of encouragement helped make this final work what it is; Pastor David Van Wagnen, for prayers and endorsement, and Ramona Palmer, manager of the Victims Resource Center of the Finger Lakes, Inc. and her husband Kurt for their support.

Special thanks to the following individuals for providing me with answers to questions that only someone in their respective professions could answer: Dr. David DiLoreto at Strong Memorial Hospital for giving me valuable information on eye injuries due to trauma and New York State Trooper Barry Chase and the N.Y.S Troopers Office of Public Information for technical help. Also, thanks to my son, Zachary Pealo. Your computer knowledge proved extremely helpful.

Names mentioned in these pages are fictitious, except those used by permission: Dr. David DiLoreto, Olivia Suhr, and Brianna Raes.

Chapter I

Pain and Reminiscence

It was an oppressively hot, humid, early August day in Marion; a small, quiet village nestled in the rolling hills of upstate New York. Not one leaf was stirring in the still, sticky early afternoon sun as the annoying high-pitched buzzing, coming from the last of the summers' cicada bugs perched high in the trees, filled the air. The towns' only thermometer, in front of the S&L bank on the corner of Main and Maple, had stood at 93 degrees and was expected to reach 97 before it started getting any cooler.

Marion has a post office, a bank, a school, a few privately owned businesses, and one, lonely traffic light, changing from green to red in perfectly timed intervals. The only major business, Finger Lakes Foods, had closed all but the can plant several years back. Like most small towns, everybody seems to know a little about everybody else, but folks here are friendly and eager to lend a hand to those in need. Up until the late '70s, Marion had mostly been a Dutch farm community, but because Rochester, nearly 25 miles to the west, had been an increasingly rougher city to live, families were opting to move to the relative quiet of Wayne County. It was this very reason why, at the age of 14, Marty's parents had decided to move there in the spring of 1987. It is in this well manicured, rural community that the young woman would learn the devastating consequences of one poor choice.

. . .

Marty Van Dorn was face down on the bathroom rug when she started to wake up. Wake up was not quite the correct terminology for it, more like regained consciousness. An involuntary moan escaped her as she tried, in vain, to open her eyes. "Oh, my God; I'm blind!" she managed. Slowly and painfully, she raised her head, willing herself not to think about the feel of the wet carpet fibers peeling away from her face. The moist, sticky sensation, coupled with that sound; the one a roller makes when applying a second coat of paint to a wall, turned her stomach and she was afraid that she was going to lose the little she had eaten for lunch. She knew exactly what that sound was and she was terrified. Blood. Her blood. "But, how much have I lost?" she thought. This question was immediately followed by a second. How long have I been here? Light and vivid colors began to fill her field of vision and even though it was blurry, she was finally able to see. Marty blinked. She blinked, again. Something was wrong.

It didn't take long for Marty to realize that she could not see out of her left eye at all. As her vision slowly came into focus, she looked over towards the window and could see the angle that the sunlight shone in. She estimated the time to be around 2 o'clock. That meant that she could not have been out

14

for too long. She remembered coming upstairs just after 1 o'clock when this had happened. Just what did happen?

Marty was in tremendous pain. Every part of her body was throbbing. Her head was pounding and her mind cloudy, but she knew she wanted to get up, needed to get up. Yet, even in her diminished state of mind, she realized that she could not just stand up and walk. She was going to need some leverage in order to do so. Marty gripped the plush fibers as tightly as she could and began to pull herself along the royal blue rug, making her way towards the tub. What usually took only seconds to perform was seemingly taking forever. After a few minutes, Marty was able to reach the tub and gently lift herself to a seated position on the edge of it. Even the slightest movement brought forth pain however, with a great deal of effort and determination, she made it.

The room was spinning before her and the dizzying feeling nearly made her fall over. She closed her eye. After a few moments rest, the nauseating feeling went away and the young woman attempted to stand. Excruciating pain in her lower right leg prevented her from accomplishing this and she screamed in agony. Seeing stars, she came back down, hard, onto the edge of the tub and nearly fell backwards into it. Arms flailing, she somehow managed to regain her balance. She sat there waiting for the pain to subside before trying to figure out her next move. She looked down at her leg. It was swollen and turning a lovely shade of purple starting midway below her knee. Her foot was turned grotesquely outward. It was obviously broken. Still, she needed to see what else was wrong with her. The only way, she felt, to properly assess the damage done to her was to be able to see her reflection in the mirror. For this she needed to stand and stand she would.

The pain she was experiencing accomplished something important. It brought Marty fully back to consciousness. The fog was gone. Now she could focus fully on the task at hand: survival. She also understood that her screaming accomplished something equally as important. No one came running up the stairs. That meant that he was gone and she was alone. That was good. She needed time.

Marty's second attempt at standing went much better than the first, but not without causing her severe pain. Her grandmother once told her when she was younger that it was good to feel pain. She said that you knew you were still alive if you felt pain. Her grandmother was no longer feeling any pain. Marty managed a slight smile thinking to herself that she must be more alive than anyone she knew, because she never knew this much, or this intense pain, in her life. Gingerly, she slid to the right towards the foot of the tub where it butted against the wall. Then, with her right hand, she reached up and gripped the solid oak towel rack. At this point, she didn't really have a plan in mind. She just wanted to be vertical.

After tugging hard, to test whether it was going to be able to hold her weight, Marty determined that she would be able to pull herself up. She, then, took a moment to think about how to

16

safely become erect. Marty placed her left foot on the floor, squarely, against the base of the tub, grabbed hold of the towel rack as tight as she could, and gave herself a silent "three count." On three, she was pulling herself up with all she had. Her ribs immediately started screaming for her to cease. She screamed back at them, refusing to give in to the pain. Colorful spots danced in her field of vision as the pain in her chest increased. She believed she knew why. She believed her ribs were broken.

Marty felt she was going to pass out. She was at the point between standing and falling over; straining, but not gaining any ground. She felt herself slipping away. She knew that there wasn't much time or strength left in her; that she would lose her grip, sending her crashing to the floor, or worse. A fall in her compromised condition could have been fatal. She pictured herself falling backward into the porcelain trough and splitting her head open. The sight in her minds' eye renewed her strength.

Mustering everything she had and with an almost primitive grunt, Marty closed her eye and gave one final pull. She felt herself moving by degrees, inching upward, until she was standing erect on her left foot with her right leg slightly bent at the knee in front of her. A rush of blood went to her head. She became nauseous and extremely dizzy. Marty leaned against the wall, heart pounding, and waited for the feeling to subside. After a minute, with the pain only a dull ache, she was able to open her eye. She pumped her fist, slightly, relieved about her mini-accomplishment.

It was only a few "paces" to the vanity and, more importantly, the etched mirror above it. She knew that she was going to have to hop, causing her more pain and possible further injury, but she rationalized that she needed to know exactly what those injuries were. Just how bad were they.

Guarding her ribs by placing her left arm tightly against her side, she took her first small hop. She had to place her right hand against the wall in order to steady herself, but the pain wasn't as bad as she expected it to be. She took a longer hop and felt a twinge on her left side; however, it was nothing she felt she had to worry about. Two more quick hops and she was able to grab onto the edge of the vanity. Gripping it with both hands to steady herself, she slowly moved into position in front of the sink. Then she raised her head to look at herself in the mirror. With tears in her eyes, Marty Van Dorn stared painfully into the glass oracle aghast at the image reflecting back at her.

.   .   .

Marty's mother had named her Madeline nearly thirty-three years ago after her favorite, if not most gentle, aunt. However, even at a young age she hated the antiquated name and asked friends and family alike to call her Marty. As a child, Marty was a beautiful girl. She grew up to be an even more beautiful woman. A lean five feet seven inches, she had the loveliest green eyes, perfect creamy complexion, and long flowing

18

red hair with a wonderful sheen when the sunlight danced upon it. Even in her young teens, Marty turned a great deal of heads and not only those of the opposite sex. She had the natural beauty that other young ladies found highly disturbing and they were all envious of her. When she would ride her eighteen speed canary yellow Scott mountain bike into town to pick up a few things for her mother at Papa Pagollo's market on the north edge of town, most conversations and street games would cease.

Marty wasn't just another pretty face in a pair of tight-fitting stone washed Levi's. She had the intelligence and personality to go along with her obvious good looks. She was on the honor roll in each of her four years of high school and wound up graduating in June of '91 third out of a class of nearly 110. Yet, as intimidating as she sounded, young Marty was always friendly, giving a "Hi, guys" and bright smile to everyone she passed by. The girl could easily have been a force to be reckoned with, however, Marty simply chose to be nice to all, even to those other girls who had been exceptionally nasty to her.

Marty was especially kind to the "little" mentally challenged girl who lived a couple of houses down from her. And it was this girl Marty was thinking of and not her own agony. She always thought about Peggy when thunderstorms approached. As she looked out of her bathroom window towards the west, she could see that one was forming. It was still a ways off, but she could see the cumulus clouds taking shape high in the atmosphere, miles away. If Marty had been able to see the news flashes on TV, she would have known that there was a storm

19

warning in effect for the area until 6 pm.

Marty felt sorry for Peggy Thornton and had a great deal of compassion for her. Every day after school, once her homework was finished and the house picked up, she would walk over and spend some quality time with "little, Peggy". Peggy hadn't been little because of her age. She was twenty the summer before Marty started her senior year in high school. Peggy was little because she had been a pudgy, four feet three inches tall and severely afflicted with Down Syndrome, which had left her with the mentality of an average four year old. Yet, for all the problems this young, mentally challenged woman was faced with, she always looked forward to seeing Marty and greeted her each day with a smile. Peggy could not tell time, but she always seemed to know when Marty was going to visit. She would either be waiting for Marty in the yard as she came walking up the street, or just coming out of her house. It didn't seem to matter to her what the weather was like, either. She was always there. And always, always there was that big, bright smile.

Peggy loved Marty and Marty loved Peggy. Marty could not understand how other kids could be so cruel as to call Peggy, and those like her, terribly mean names and act malicious towards them. Peggy was the sweetest, most innocent person she had ever met, always talking about the Lord and saying that she wouldn't always look like this. "Someday," she said, "I'm going to be pretty and have wings." Marty would sometimes cry and have to turn her head away thinking about what Peggy said and Peggy would hug Marty and tell her it was going to be okay.

20

That would astound Marty. Peggy would talk about her affliction the way others talk about the weather. To Marty, Peggy seemed to be the strong one, at least in faith, and she the weak. So, in Marty's eyes, she had learned as much from Peggy as Peggy did from her, although most of what Marty taught her would usually have to be taught, again. Peggy always had a great deal of difficulty retaining information, but Marty was always patient with her, giving plenty of encouragement and lots of hugs. Peggy would always hug back with huge, over-exaggerated pats on the back and say to her, "I love you, Marty."

Because boys were afraid to ask her out for fear of rejection and most girls felt threatened by her and, therefore, wouldn't talk to her, Peggy wonderfully filled the void of companionship in Marty's life. For different reasons, they were both social outcasts who simply found each other and Marty was fine with that.

That summer, Marty's parents, Bill and Julia Leonard, planned to take their only child with them on vacation to the Adirondack Mountains. They usually went to exotic places and left Marty with Julia's sister, Jackie, who owned a horse farm near Binghamton off Route 81. But, because they realized that they were only going to have Marty two more summers before she headed off to college, they both agreed to take her to the places where they knew she had liked to go. Marty loved the mountains. She liked camping, fishing, climbing "Whiteface" and never seemed to tire from the miles of trails her parents took her on. She even enjoyed the time when she had been badly bitten by black flies. That was the June she turned eleven. It was quiet and peaceful and all of her troubles seemed to melt away like the snow on the mountain peaks in springtime.

Marty became quite good at imitating the various kinds of birds that always seemed to be more plentiful in the mountains, including the sad song of the mourning doves. She would always laugh when the bird she was imitating would take wing to find out where the new "intruder" of its territory was located so it could confront and scare the trespasser away. Then, when the bird would realize the culprit was Marty, it would fly back to its nest. Marty pictured the bird going back to its mate and saying "That was the biggest one-of-us I ever saw and I'm not messing with it."

Marty told Peggy the day before she and her family left for the mountains that she was going away for a while, but that she would be back soon to play with her. She felt that she wouldn't have been able to explain to Peggy what vacations were or the concept of two weeks, so she kept it as simple as possible. The reaction was immediate and took Marty by surprise. Peggy became visibly distraught. She started to cry and told Marty that she was making it up.

"Marty not want play Peggy none more," she sobbed, tears running down her face.

Marty was shocked at how quickly Peggy went from being happy to borderline hysterics in a matter of seconds. She

22

had never seen Peggy like that, before. "No, Peggy. That's not true. I have to go away with my mommy and daddy for a while, but I'll be back."

"No. NO." Peggy shouted. "Marty not love Peggy." And she got up and ran into the house, crying hysterically.

Marty started to run after her, but quickly decided that it just might make matters worse and stopped dead in her tracks. She tried to reassure Peggy that she was going to be back soon and didn't know what else she could say. Marty watched as Peggy opened the door, trip on the step leading into the house, and slam it shut behind her. Mrs. Thornton, knowing that Marty would not intentionally hurt her daughter, came to the door and asked her what had happened. Marty expressed to her that she was trying to explain to Peggy that her family was going on vacation and would not be back for a while. She also told her how Peggy thought that she had no longer wanted to play with her.

"I know, dearie. You go home and don't worry about it. I'll make a nice chocolate cake for Peggy and talk to her when she calms down."

Sharon Thornton liked Marty a great deal and respected her for taking the time to interact with Peggy. She was skeptical the first couple of days that Marty came to the house, watching the two of them from the living room window, constantly, with a mother's protective eyes. However, it didn't take Marty long to put on the natural charm and, in no time, Sharon felt comfortable with her. She could see that this young girl was truly genuine and, in time, became as fond of Marty as Peggy was.

Sharon Thornton was a short, thin woman, but she was far from frail. She was a five foot two inch stick of dynamite that very few were willing to take on. It seemed that she was always arguing with someone or some agency. She spent a better part of the last twenty years fighting with schools and government agencies to get her daughter the assistance she needed. Neither, was she afraid to quarrel with the teens in the neighborhood that thought it acceptable to tease Peggy. Make no mistake, Sharon Thornton was a great advocate for her daughter and loved her dearly.

Yet, the stress of raising a mentally challenged child was clearly visible and took its toll on her. She was only fifty-one, but her hair had turned prematurely white. There were only a few strands left of her natural auburn. Sharon never bothered with hair coloring to cover it. She simply accepted it. She also had dark circles under her eyes and wrinkles that even the best make-up could not hide.

Marty walked back to her house deeply saddened. She didn't feel good about how she had conducted herself. "I never should have said anything directly to Peggy. I should have just told Mrs. Thornton about my vacation and let her figure out how best to handle it." She told her mother.

"It'll be all right. You had no idea that it was going to

affect her like that," Julia stated, trying to make her daughter feel better.

True. She honestly didn't believe at the time that telling Peggy about her trip would make her react in such a negative way. Marty thought about telling her parents she didn't want to go, but knew how much they were looking forward to spending the time with her. Besides that, she knew that her parents had already taken the time off from work and rented the cabins, up north. No, she had no choice. She had to go. Peggy was just going to have to find her own way to deal with this.

Always thinking on the positive side, Marty's thoughts then turned to what she could get Peggy while she was in the mountains. She thought about getting her something nice to wear for the fall, a cool sweatshirt, maybe. I'll bet she would like that, she thought. Immediately, she began to feel better about going. Once Peggy saw that Marty hadn't shunned her, that she even had a gift for her, everything would be as it was before she left.

It was the last time Marty ever saw her.

.　.　.

After an eventful two weeks of hiking, fishing, and canoeing, the Leonard family returned to the normalcy of Marion. Bill and Julia were glad to be getting home. Julia was forty-four and Bill was pushing fifty. The two weeks of running around what seemed to be half of the state had definitely tired them out. Marty, however was in good spirits. Not only was the trip educational and invigorating for the new high school senior, Marty felt somehow rejuvenated and more alive than she had in a long time. She had a wonderful time with her parents, but, at the time, her thoughts were focused on the little gift bag on her lap and the young woman whom it was for.

Marty could not wait to share all of her experiences with the woman/child. She was trying to figure out how to tell Peggy about how her father nearly tipped the canoe over while trying to help her mother net the three-pound bass she caught on Cranberry Lake. Then, about the time a huge black bear and young cub strolled past their cabin window, sniffing for any tasty morsels that may have been left out. Marty's parents were always extremely careful, keeping a tight lid on all food items and garbage cans for just that reason.

"I'm going to need a vacation from my vacation. My back is killing me," Bill said as he pulled into the driveway.

Looking up at the graying sky, Julia stated, "Me, too. Looks like there's a storm coming. I'm glad we beat it home."

Marty jumped out, barely waiting for her father to put the '89 Olds in park. "Bye, mom. 'Love ya, dad." She yelled to her parents as she sprinted across the yard.

Marty's agreement had been to help her parents unpack as soon as she gave Peggy her gifts. They gave her a half hour to do so, but with the storm moving in, it looked like it might be a little longer than that. They, too, felt that what their daughter had been doing for Peggy was commendable. She ran towards Peggy's house carrying the gift bag with the 'I Love NY' sweatshirt and a jar of real maple syrup. Off in the distance she saw a streak of lightning followed by a long clap of thunder.

Peggy wasn't waiting in the yard for her as she usually did nearly every day since mid-April when the weather finally started to turn nice. This did not surprise her because Peggy wasn't expecting her this time of the day and she could tell that a pretty good storm was coming in from the west. She stopped running once she reached the Thornton's driveway, not even slightly winded. Something wasn't quite right, but she hadn't been able to place a finger on it. The clouds rolled in and a small drop of rain landed on her cheek. Lightning flashed across the sky, followed by another long clap of thunder. This one was much closer. As the storm moved in, Marty slowed her pace.

Halfway down the driveway, Marty realized what seemed out of place to her. Not one toy in the yard. That was odd because even on the most miserable of days there were always toys, most of them made by Fisher-Price, on the lawn. On that day, however, there was not as much as a piece of chalk or ball. She rationalized in her mind that, maybe, this particular storm was going to be quite bad and that the Thornton's had picked up the yard in anticipation of it. The wind picked up and it started to sprinkle. Marty walked up the steps, feeling slightly uneasy and knocked at the door.

The door opened and a somber looking Sharon Thornton greeted her. "Hello, Marty," she said, without the slightest bit of enthusiasm. "I knew you would be stopping by sometime this week."

This wasn't the way Mrs. Thornton usually addressed her and she knew something was wrong, but pressed on, anyway. "I bought some things for Peggy while I was away and would like to give them to her," she said, raising the bag to show her.

Sharon started to cry, big heaving sobs that she could not control. Gasping between syllables, she cried "Peg-gy- died- last- Sat-urday. I- c-can't- talk- right- now." She shut the door. Even with the wind howling around her, she could still hear the woman crying from inside of her home.

Marty stood in shock, still holding the gift bag in her outstretched hand. She was trying to process what she had just heard. It was as if it didn't fully register in her mind. Seconds passed and she still couldn't move. It was like her feet were welded to the steps. She was completely dumbfounded. Suddenly, she began to feel sick to her stomach and the pressure started to build inside her, just as the storm was building up around her. It took awhile, but the information given to her was properly absorbed and processed and tears started to flow down her cheeks. She felt herself losing control. Two flashes of

28

lightning in quick succession ushered in a downpour of water and Mother Nature unleashed her fury.

Even in the open air, as the torrential rain pelted her body with gigantic drops, Marty felt as if the walls were closing in on her. She dropped the bag on the steps, smashing the jar of maple syrup. In a matter of moments she felt her whole world, like the jar of syrup, was shattered. Her one and only companion had died. Her life had been parents, paperbacks, and Peggy and now Peggy had been taken from her. She turned and ran.

Marty didn't have a boyfriend. In fact, she didn't have any friends at all and she could not understand why. She was nice to everyone. Why didn't anyone like her? Lightning flashes were all around her, but Marty barely noticed them. Tears were flowing freely down her face, mixing with the rivers of water. She could taste the saltiness on her lips and tongue. She wanted to get away, but where could she go? She was home.

Suddenly, a bright flash of light filled the sky, temporarily blinding Marty. Directly above her came a long booming crack, but she never missed a step. The ground started to shake underneath her as the big oak tree in the neighbors' yard started to topple over. Marty, regaining her sight, never looked back. She just kept running, oblivious to the danger.

Marty reached her driveway at full speed and cut across the yard, heading for the front door, as the uprooted behemoth came crashing down, its top branches narrowly missing her. She turned and gave it a cursory look through her tears. She didn't care what happened to her. She almost wished it had fallen on her.

Marty's parents, who were just saying how lucky they had been to make it home before the storm, were sitting down to have a cup of tea. They felt and heard the tree come down in the lawn and were headed for the front door when it burst open. Marty, obviously distraught, came in, slammed the door shut behind her and ran straight for her room, crying hysterically. She was drenched, but too consumed with grief to care. She collapsed on her bed as her parents chased after her. They thought that the falling tree might have hurt her. They huddled around their daughter, asking her medical questions, but it would be nearly twenty minutes before Marty could tell them what was wrong.

From that day on, Marty hated thunderstorms. They would always remind her of the time she found out about Peggy's death and that she never had the chance to say good-bye. For her, there wasn't any closure. That fearsome early August storm was nearly 16 years ago to the day. It ushered in her first taste of grief; her first taste of loss, and it greatly affected her.

Marty didn't blame herself, directly, for Peggy's death. She understood that most individuals with severe Down syndrome simply did not live long, due to any number of reasons. In Peggy's case, Marty found out that she had aspirated something she had been eating the day after her family left for their vacation. It went into her lungs where it quickly turned into

30

pneumonia from which the young woman never recovered. What Marty had always wondered about, languished over, was Peggy's depressed state. Had she been distraught, thinking about what Marty told her about the vacation and it, somehow, contributed to her death? Had she been crying when she had started choking? These were questions that could never be answered.

What Marty had blamed herself, for all these years, was the way in which she and Peggy parted the last time they were together. She always felt that she should have said something different or tried to stop Peggy from going into the house in such a depressed state. She simply blamed herself for the choices she made that day. And she was blaming herself, once again, for another poor choice: agreeing to marry Roger Van Dorn.

Chapter II

Roger's Alibi

Roger Van Dorn was staring at the battered, limp body of his wife, Marty; his anger spent. He wasn't a particularly big man; an average five feet-ten, thin, except for the slight beer gut he was getting from the "lunches" at Rusty's Roost and wavy dark brown-almost black hair that was starting to thin on top. Because he had been a farmer since he could remember, growing up on his fathers' potato farm, Roger was also strong and muscular.

This time of year, he was sporting a dark, even tan that made him look a great deal like the migrant workers that came up every year from Puerto Rico to work the farms. He was also a heavy smoker, which made him look somewhat older than his 34 years. He wore only jeans and a t-shirt and usually had five or six days of facial growth. This day was no different.

The anger, which had been building up inside him for weeks, was finally unleashed on his unsuspecting wife. Roger exploded. He didn't mean to hit her that hard, initially, but once he started, he knew that he couldn't stop until she was dead. He realized that she would never forgive him, this time. She would, most assuredly, call the police and he would wind up behind bars, losing just about everything he had worked for. That just wouldn't do. Jail was not an option. He was not about to go to prison because of her.

Roger had enough of Marty's "nagging" about the bills and the endless repairs around the house that he seemed to never have any time for, and let loose on her. Why couldn't she have just kept her mouth shut about them? This would not have happened if she did what she was supposed to do, told to do, and leave him alone.

Roger was panting hard and his right hand was sore. The knuckles on his second and third fingers were split and bleeding. It had taken a great deal more effort than he thought it would. He looked down at his hand, disgusted.

"Great. Just, friggin', dandy!" he exclaimed sarcastically to no one, as he went over to the vanity to wash his cuts. He knew he was going to need a couple of bandages for them.

"Your head is a lot harder than I thought," he said sneering down at Marty. Then, he opened the medicine cabinet and took out a couple of bandages.

Not bothering with a towel, Roger dried his hands on his blood, sweat and coffee stained t-shirt and applied the bandages to his wounds. Then, he surveyed the room.

"This isn't good," he muttered.

A few blood splatters were on the cabinets, ceiling and windows and would have to be taken care of immediately. Most of it, however, was nicely contained on the rug. That would have to be removed and destroyed after he disposed of the body, but, for now, that could wait. He went downstairs to get a plastic garbage bag. No sense wasting time.

A minute later, Roger returned, thankful that all of the cleaning supplies were kept in the bathroom. He would not have to be bothered with carrying any bottles back and forth. Without giving his wife even the slightest glance, Roger went to the supply cabinets and opened one. He reached in and took out a washrag, a roll of paper towel, and the Windex. From a second cabinet, he took out a small pail and some bleach.

Stepping over Marty's legs, Roger walked, methodically, over to the tub and turned on the hot water. There was a sense of urgency, but he knew he had to keep a clear head and stay focused or he would be in danger of making mistakes. He could not afford to make mistakes. Roger poured some bleach in the bucket and placed it under the faucet. While it was filling, he opened the roll of paper towel. Time was precious. He had to get down to Rusty's for lunch with the guys. Every Friday at 2 o'clock, he had lunch with the guys and it would not be a good day to miss this one. He needed to have an alibi in case people, uniformed people, started asking serious questions about Marty's whereabouts. He needed to be seen; needed to be normal. A quick glance at his watch: 1:21. There wasn't much time.

Roger turned off the faucet and dropped the washrag into the pail. He then started washing the walls with it. He wanted to get these first before the blood had time to dry. If it did, he knew that he would have a much harder time getting it off later. He might even have to re-paint. That would have been too much work in a short amount of time. Besides that, fresh paint would immediately arouse suspicion if an investigator came to check on the house. He had watched enough "Forensic Files" on cable to know that. He was the husband. The prime suspect in any wife's disappearance was usually the husband. Roger dried the wet spots with a couple of sheets of paper towel and inspected his work.

After he was satisfied that the walls and ceiling were clean, Roger took the window cleaner and sprayed the mirror and windows with it. No time to waste. He had to scrub hard at times, especially when cleaning the last window, because the blood had already started to dry. Roger checked his watch again. 1:47. He was cutting it close. There was absolutely no way he was going to be able to dispose of the body and get the rug out of there. It was going to have to wait until he got back. He emptied the bucket down the tub drain and threw the washrag and used paper towels into the garbage bag. Then, stepping over Marty once again, he placed the bleach, pail, and roll of paper towel back into the cabinets. He flipped the bag over his shoulder and surveyed the room. Satisfied, he left, leaving the bottle of Windex on the vanity.

36

In his haste, Roger did not look down at his wife who was lying motionless, face down on the floor. If he had, he may have noticed that she wasn't dead. She was breathing, shallowly, but she was still very much alive. Had he seen that, he would have remedied it, quickly. Lucky for her, he didn't.

Roger knew that he didn't have enough time to freshen up properly, so he dabbed on some Stetson cologne and put on a clean, buttoned-down, dark blue shirt over the t-shirt he had been wearing. He thought that it would hide the blood spatters, as well as those old coffee stains nicely. He picked up a comb from off of the dresser and ran out the front doorway and into the sweltering heat of the early August day.

Halfway to the driveway, Roger realized that he had left the keys to the pick-up on the kitchen table.

"Damn."

He sprinted back to the house, flung open the door and went in. He ran through the living area, past the flight of stairs and into the kitchen. Grabbing the keys off of the table, Roger turned and made a dash for the front door. He was nearly to it when he thought he heard something. Had that been a moan, or was he hearing things because he had been in such a hurry? With one hand on the doorknob, Roger cocked an ear toward the stairway and listened, intently. After a moment, he glanced at his watch. 1:52. He took a brief look at the stairs and decided that he must have been hearing things and went out, not bothering to lock the door. No one bothers anybody out here. There was no way, he thought to himself as he ran to his truck, that she could survive a beating like the one he had given her. He must be going crazy. Given the circumstances, he didn't think that was a stretch.

Upstairs, in the bathroom, Marty moaned for the second time.

Roger opened the door to his fire engine red '05, Chevy Silverado. Hastily, he jumped up into the cab and started the big V-6. He pumped the gas pedal a couple of times, revving the engine, before he threw it in gear and headed out of the driveway. He was in a hurry to get to his destination, but he still had the sense not to leave any rubber on the pavement, as he left. It would not have been a good time to draw attention. Shifting into second, Roger headed down the road with a smug look on his face. He was fairly confident, under the circumstances, with how well the clean-up had turned out. Things seemed to be going just fine.

Roger, smartly, whipped his truck into a vacant parking space at Rusty's in front of the blue neon Bud Light sign and glanced at the dashboard clock. 2:04. Not bad at all. No one was going to question him. In fact, his best friend, Matt Tillman, was just pulling up behind him. He looked into the rearview mirror, took out the comb from his back pocket, and started combing his thick mane with it.

Matt stepped out of his Ford F-150 and strolled up to Rogers' truck. He was an overweight, balding forty-two year old, with massive arms and a deep, rugged voice that most children found intimidating. He was dressed in jeans held tight around his waist by a thick leather belt and blue suspenders with a t-shirt that read "Gone Crazy! Be back, soon." Sweat was pouring off the big man's forehead as he strolled up to Rogers' pick-up.

"Quit primping, pretty boy and let's get something to eat," he told Roger, a huge grin on his face.

"You're just jealous you old Q-ball."

"Hey, how'd you get those?" Matt asked, pointing to his bandages on Rogers' knuckles. "Cut yourself doing the dishes, again."

"Yah. How'd you get those scratches on your arm? Were ya tryin' to milk your pregnant cat?" Roger poked back, stepping out of the truck.

They both laughed and Matt gave Roger the biggest bear hug he had ever had. They shook hands and headed for the door.

"Hey. How'd you know fluffy was pregnant? You're not the father, are you?"

Roger laughed. The light banter was good for him. It had loosened him up, a bit. He felt confident that he was going to be able to pull it off. With one of the only friends he had left in the world close behind him, Roger walked into the bar; a huge smile on his face.

.   .   .

Roger had lived all of his life on the 163-acre Van Dorn homestead on the far southeast corner of town. It had been in the family for six generations, dating back to 1842. His great-great-great grandfather Isaac Van Dorn built the original portion of the home and barn across the road (before there even was a road) with his own two hands. He used whole trees in the construction process, securing them with large wooden pegs. Some of the trees used still have bark on them, to this day.

Van Dorn Road, named after the family, runs north south, cutting between the house and the barns. It curves, sharply, at nearly a perfect ninety degrees about two hundred and fifty yards to the south. It had been paved with several twists and turns, following the existing cart paths, back in the '30s, to accommodate all of the farms on the road. Paving it this way also prevented valuable farmland from being bisected. Along many stretches, the road is lined with huge oak and maple trees, making it one of the nicest drives in all of Marion.

The old farmhouse, itself, sits at the base of a small hill, overlooking a spacious valley of rich muck land where, at one

40

time, there had been a small lake. The soil is dark and rich, which makes it perfect for growing just about anything. The property was beautifully landscaped, having several gardens loaded with Daffodils, Irises, Tulips, and several different kinds of Hostas. Lilac and flowering crab apple trees dotted the yard as well. From early spring until late in the fall there had always been something in bloom. The two giant oak trees that his great-great grandfather, Jacob had planted stood like sentinels on either side of the driveway, near the edge of the road.

The original barn is nearly 90 feet long by 60 wide and sits to the northwest of the home at a sharp angle to allow for a better view of the valley. After 165 years, it is still as straight as when Isaac built it.

Since then, the homestead went through a number of addition changes. Two bedrooms were added to the home in 1886 and the dining area was built in 1919, just after his great grandfather had come back from the War, in Europe. His Father, John, added a wrap-around porch and built another large pole barn in the early '70s. John owned it for nearly forty years (after his father had died from injuries sustained in a freak plowing accident that completely severed his leg back in '56) before letting his son take over in '94.

In the years he had owned the farm, John built a successful potato business, but felt that it had been time to slow down and let the next generation take over. Besides, he believed that his son would finally become responsible since he had a young wife to care for and transferred the deed over to Roger as a late wedding present. Almost immediately, John regretted that decision.

It wasn't that Roger didn't know how to grow potatoes. He had learned from his father when to plant, spray for insects, irrigate (when necessary), and harvest. Roger just didn't have good business sense or know how to talk to people. He had a quick temper, a tendency to make others angry, and always needed to have things his own way. He destroyed friendships in the business that had taken his father years to cultivate; whether it was employees, truck drivers, or buyers.

Very few would deal with Roger, directly. He alienated himself from nearly everyone, including his father. Some would whisper behind John's back, complaining about Roger. Others, especially those farmhands that had been steady employees, were bold enough to tell him just how bad things had become since his son took over. John would get upset and eat Rolaids as if they were candy, but would not allow himself to show it, outwardly. What could he do? He no longer owned the farm.

Another flaw that Roger had was his tendency to procrastinate when it came to equipment maintenance. Three years earlier, the International Harvester sprayer had broken down as he was starting the second field. The burned bearings created a great deal of blue-gray smoke. It wouldn't have happened if Roger had ensured they were greased, properly. Roger became angry and started swearing. He walked away and

42

let it sit there for several weeks, untouched, until his farmhands noticed that insects had been eating the leaves off of the plants. By the time Roger finally repaired the sprayer, he had lost nearly a third of his crop. Three of his farmhands quit on the spot. They had had enough and were not about to listen to any more of Rogers' tirades. That was all right with Roger. With so much of his yield gone, he was going to have to lay a couple of them off anyway. He wouldn't have been able to pay their wages.

After eleven years of bad decisions, bad weather, and just plain bad luck, 2006 had been a make or break year for Roger. His livelihood was going to depend on the outcome of the harvest and he did everything in his power to ensure a bountiful one. He woke up early every day and put in long hours. He was under a great deal of stress, but everything had been good until that point in the growing season. The weather and equipment were cooperative and the plants were healthy. If August were going to be as good as June and July, he would be home free. He only wished that his father could have been around to see it.

John had a stroke a couple of years back that left him paralyzed on his entire left side. He could no longer raise his arm and his face drooped noticeably on that side as well. Talking and swallowing had become extremely difficult and he was, therefore, placed on a puree diet. Many people talked behind Rogers' back, saying that he was the cause of it; that his father had been sick over the mismanagement of the farm. He heard some of the comments, but chose to ignore them. There were other factors as well, such as high blood pressure, but overall they had been right.

The stress was too much for him. Because John had a service connected injury, stemming from a North Korean bullet he took in his right leg back in '52, he had been eligible to be placed in the Veterans Hospital in Canandaigua, about twenty miles south.

Initially, John, as well as the doctors performing the surgery, feared that he was going to lose the leg. However, quick reactions by the field medics and the surgeons at the M*A*S*H unit where he was lifted, were able to save it. An eight-inch jagged scar, running lengthwise down his thigh, along with the noticeable limp, were constant reminders of that fateful day. Since he didn't lose the leg and had been able to walk again, John was almost thankful for it. It was his ticket out of that hellish place. From then on, he never complained about his injury and had always been proud of the Purple Heart he received and wore it every year, faithfully, in the Memorial Day parade.

Roger had made it a point to visit his father twice a year. It was too damned depressing for him to see his dad more often than that and he always dreaded the times that he did. That had been all right with John. He did not want to see his son, anyway.

Many years, John blamed himself for how Roger had turned out. When he was a child growing up, John and his family didn't have money for any luxuries and were, barely, able to scrape by. The depression and war years hit everyone hard, but it seemed to have created even greater hardships for area farmers. John went without many of the necessities that the current generation takes for granted. Once the farm, under his competent

44

management, turned a profit and prospered in the '60s and '70s he felt that he needed to provide for his son the niceties that he and his siblings never had growing up. John's intent was not to spoil his son, but that is exactly what had been the result. He just wanted the best for his unappreciative son.

. . .

Matt and Roger headed straight to the bar. They both pulled out a high backed stool and sat down. They both ordered a bottle of Coors from longtime owner Rusty "Nails" Nailstrom. They were real men, and there were two things real men didn't do; sit at tables (unless with someone of the opposite sex) or drink light beer.

Rusty placed two coasters on the bar and placed a beer on each one. He was a short, rather thin fellow with a thick, almost white Colonel Sander's goatee and equally full head of white hair. Even though the man was in his mid '70s, he had more energy than most men half his age. On many occasions, he had been asked when he planned on retiring and his reply had always been the same.

"They are going to have to carry my dead body out from behind the bar."

Mr. Nailstrom built the place in 1958, just over the

Marion town border in Palmyra on Route 21. Since then, he had put everything he had into it. He loved the bar and just about everything that went along with it; the people, the summer softball league, the crack of a well broken rack at the pool table, and even the occasional fight when someone who, evidently, couldn't hold his booze would start something. A great deal of his life had been spent behind that bar. In fact, there were few patrons who came in the place that could remember a time when Rusty's wasn't there.

A few years back, he briefly, thought about selling the place and moving south, but at the last minute decided not to. He couldn't do it. There were too many memories for him to be able to just pack up and leave. His heart was here.

Out of habit, Roger grabbed a menu off of the counter rack, but he already knew what he was going to order. He always ordered the same thing; a deluxe cheeseburger with extra mayo and side of onion rings. Matt was trying to lose weight, but there was absolutely no way he was going to order a garden salad while he was with the guys. That was another thing that real men didn't do. He had his mind set on having a dozen Buffalo chicken wings and a double order of fries.

Holding a damp cloth, Rusty walked over to the two of them. He wiped the counter off in front of them, giving Roger a brief look of disdain and said, "What'll it be, gentlemen?"

Rusty was one of the many who believed that Roger had

been the cause of Johns' stroke. John was not only a valued customer, but a longtime friend, as well. He had been one of the first to enter the bar when it had opened almost a half century ago, and it was one of the last places he had gone before having the stroke. John confided in him. He told Rusty that he had regretted giving the farm to his son. He also said that he had truly felt sorry for Rogers' wife, Madeline, (He never could get used to calling her Marty) for having put up with him "all this time." He was thankful, at least, that he didn't have any grandchildren to worry about. Twenty minutes later, John had left, leaving his beer untouched, on the bar. Rusty noted that John hadn't looked good that night. He seemed extremely tired and was short of breath. His skin looked ashen in color. Rusty regretted not saying anything about that to him, because the next morning, as he went out to bring in the morning paper, John had collapsed in his driveway.

Matt said, "I guess I'll have an order of those Buffalo wings and give me a couple of orders of fries with that will ya, Rusty?"

"Sure thing," he said, taking down the order on a small note pad. He half turned to Roger and asked, "What about you, Rog?"

"I guess I'll just have my usual, Rusty. No sense messing with a good thing. I'll also take another one of these, too," he said, raising his beer bottle. Matt liked the sound of that.

"I could use another one of those, myself, Rus," Matt said, draining the rest of his first one for emphasis.

Rusty headed toward the kitchen to give their orders to his wife, Jean. She made the best hamburgers around, but because of her arthritis, she wasn't as quick as she had been in her younger days. Few dared to complain, however. She was tough for pushing 70 and wouldn't hesitate to come out from the back with a hot skillet and smack the idiot complainer square on the head. More than a few had run out of the place with Jean trailing behind, waiving a frying pan and yelling profanity, because they had told her to hurry it up. No one, not even Rusty, would mess with her when she got like that. All he could say was "Look out, boys. Here she comes."

Rusty returned with the two beers before Roger had finished his first one. He took a long swig and set the bottle, empty, onto the counter. Chalk up another thing that real men didn't do: drink beer from a glass. He was feeling pretty good and had actually forgotten about Marty when Matt turned and asked, "So. How's that pretty wife of yours?'

Chapter III

Pain and Reminiscence II

Tears. A stinging, almost burning sensation as the salty wetness washed over her grotesque, misshapen eye. Marty didn't want to cry; didn't want to give Roger the satisfaction, but she was powerless to stop them. Normally, she would not have considered crying a sign of weakness. However, in this instance, she thought of it as conceding a loss to him. She had not prepared herself for seeing something this bad, and to her, this ugly. A combination of disbelief, coupled with actually seeing the devastating results, sent her over the edge. Lowering her head, Marty wept, bitterly, letting her tears fall freely into the sink. She allowed herself a few minutes to get it all out of her system, before regaining her composure and raising her head, once again.

"Why? What have I done to deserve this?" she asked herself, gaining the courage to look back into the mirror.

As Marty stared in disbelief at the repulsive features that less than an hour previous had been her pretty face, she wondered how she could have let things get as bad as they had become. At one time she had been a strong, confident young woman. How could she have allowed Roger to beat her, like this? Why did she let him have so damned much control of her life? And the most important question needing to be answered—

where was he now?

The most urgent priority had been to assess the damage done to her. The initial shock of what she had seen in the mirror was over. It was time to inventory everything that was seriously wrong with her; those injuries that needed to be treated immediately, as well as the superficial ones that could, possibly, wait. Broken bones and deep lacerations would need to be addressed. Precious moments were being wasted. Roger might be returning at any time and she wanted to be ready for him, when he did. She gazed, purposefully, into the mirror, taking a deep, cleansing breath. "All right, let's get to it," she said aloud and went to work.

Marty realized at once why she could not see out of her left eye. The tissue around it was black and swollen, preventing her from opening it. A moderate amount of blood was slowly running down her cheek, from the corner, but she could not tell if it was only coming from the two-inch gash above the eye, or if the eye itself, was also bleeding. She reached for the hand towel on the rack and tried in vain to wipe away the blood. She felt that she needed to get a better visual, but it had been too painful.

Marty felt a throbbing pain at the top of her head and lowered it to get a better look. She found a huge clump of hair missing. The spot where it had been was raw and glistening with fresh blood. Swirls of blood were also coagulating on the side of her face—the right side where she had been lying in it on the floor. Turning on the cold water, she placed the towel under the faucet to dampen it. With it, she was able to wipe most of the blood off her face. She discovered no new cuts in the area she had cleaned. Marty rinsed the towel under the faucet, turning the water a nice shade of pink, and placed it, gently on the top of her head, with her right hand. It was too painful to raise her left. The cool cloth had a soothing effect and she sighed with the relief it brought.

Marty continued with her assessment. Her upper lip was split in two places. Fat didn't nearly describe it. It was more than double its normal size. Her jaw was throbbing with every beat of her heart. Using her facial muscles, she was able to raise her lip enough to reveal a gaping hole where her two front teeth had been. This hurt more than her broken bones. She had had a beautiful smile. Marty stifled a new onslaught of tears and continued her self-examination.

It caused her some discomfort to move her jaw, but Marty didn't feel that it was broken, unlike her nose. That she knew was broken. It had an almost comical "S" shaped curve starting at the bridge. It may have been funny had it been on someone else's face, but this was her face and it was a mess. Mary Kay and Revlon would not be able to cover that.

Marty suppressed the tears and continued with the evaluation of the rest of her body. She already knew that the right leg was broken. The slightest bump still brought forth a great amount of pain. She knew that that was going to pose a major problem if Roger decided to come home within the next hour, or so. She knew she wouldn't have been able to get away from him if he came home angry. Marty tried not to think about it.

From the moment that she pulled herself up with the aid of the towel rack her husband had finally installed several weeks back, Marty believed that she had some broken ribs, as well. Until that moment, she hadn't noticed that she was taking short, rather labored breaths. She was astounded at that, but there were too many things to focus on, at one time. Slowly and painfully, she lifted what had remained of her, blood-spattered, floral print blouse. The right sleeve was completely torn off and the left didn't have far to go before it, too, would come off. The top three buttons had also been ripped free, nearly exposing her breasts. She had always gone without wearing a bra this time of year, as long as she was only going to be walking around the house. It was much more comfortable. She couldn't lift the blouse high enough so she decided to take it off. Marty unbuttoned the remaining two buttons using only her right hand, gently slipped it off of her shoulders, and let it fall to the floor.

Several good-sized bruises were forming on her left side and abdomen where Roger had kicked her repeatedly. And, as she feared, Marty also had a couple of broken ribs. The raised area above her left breast was a sure sign that bones had been fractured, but she didn't believe that she had any internal injuries. She did not feel any internal pain associated with ruptured organs, but she wasn't about to rule it completely out, either. It was more than possible that some of the bruising on her abdomen had been caused by internal injuries. She would have to monitor those, closely. Marty couldn't see anything else wrong with her, at the time, but gave herself a second look in case she missed something.

Marty was satisfied that she had not overlooked anything. For all the injuries she had sustained, she believed that things could have been much worse. Disfigured and in need of medical attention, she felt determined to wait until she had confronted Roger, before calling for an ambulance. Immobilizing the right leg was her top priority, but most of the other injuries, such as the laceration above her eye and broken nose, would have to wait. She knew that there was almost nothing she could do for her broken ribs, either, other than guard them by placing her arm tightly at her side. At least she had all of her faculties. She was still sharp of mind. That, she knew, still made her dangerous, just like in the book "The Most Dangerous Game." And she had intended on showing Roger just how dangerous an intelligent woman could be. She had been the prey; the hunted, but she had no intentions of remaining that way. She turned her pain into anger.

Marty knew that she was going to have to be extremely careful and calculate every move. She could not afford to further injure herself and one mistake could be disastrous. A lung could be punctured or an artery severed. If that happened, death could come within minutes.

Why hadn't she listened to her father or her most trusted

friend, Stephanie? They both told her to leave Roger after the first time he hit her, several years back, but her heart couldn't allow it. It wasn't that she still had love for the man. Strange as it may sound, Marty simply felt sorry for Roger. At the time, she felt that, no matter how hard he tried, nothing seemed to be going right for him. The harvest, that year, was a tremendous disappointment, because the sprayer had broken down earlier in the growing season. She honestly understood the reason behind his going off the deep end and learned to accept his tirades, even when others could not. Once the pressure was gone and they were making a decent living, she had been confident that Roger would treat her better. In the meantime, Marty did everything in her power to make life as easy as possible for him so that he wouldn't feel the need to strike her.

When Bill heard that Roger had struck his precious daughter, he wanted to take matters into his own hands. He was furious. Marty begged her father not to confront him, however. She knew that her father was no match for Roger, but, more importantly, Marty didn't want her father to become sick over it. Reluctantly, Bill backed away.

Yet, even after months had passed, he felt the need to, at least, speak his mind. It ate at him like a cancer. He could feel his blood pressure rising every time he thought about it. He knew that it was only a matter of time before Roger would strike Marty, again. Once a man had struck a woman, for any reason, he believed the man would continue doing so. He had wanted to put a stop to that. He never got the chance.

54

On a snowy, frigid day, a day that reminds everyone after the January thaw that it is, indeed, still winter, Bill went out to shovel the walkway for Julia. The forecast had been calling for nearly a foot and a half of the thick, heavy white stuff in the area and Julia thought it would be a good idea to pick up a few things at the store before it had became too miserable to drive. Bill, always the gentleman, wanted to make sure that the walkway was clear for his wife since it had been coming down faster than before she left. He was worried about her driving in the near blizzard conditions, but he knew that she would be safely home, shortly. With that in mind, Bill picked up his pace.

When Julia arrived home a short time later, she found the shovel at the edge of the driveway. She looked up and saw Bill face down on the steps in front of the entrance door. He had tried to make it back to the house before he collapsed. She dropped the bags that she had been carrying and ran the last few steps to him. Bill felt cold. He wasn't breathing. But, she noticed that he was only covered with a thin layer of snow, which meant that he had not been there for too long. Julia quickly ran into the house and dialed those three numbers and then, went back outside. She tried to drag her husband into the house, but it was futile. He was a big man and she was simply not strong enough. When the paramedics arrived six minutes later, Julia was huddled next to the man whom she had spent the last thirty-seven years of her life with, sobbing. They had been through so much together and she was not about to leave him as he made his transition to the next life.

Yet, it wasn't her father whom Marty had been thinking about at the time. It was Stephanie. She missed not seeing or talking to her. Marty knew the reason, too. She had not heard from Stephanie in quite some time because she did not like Roger.

Stephanie Stafford hadn't liked Roger since they were kids in high school. His arrogance and endless desire to control nearly every aspect of Marty's life, was appalling to her. He made her cringe. Over time, she had had enough of his jealous behavior and stopped going to visit her. Marty, of course, had not been allowed to visit her very often, either. Even the phone calls diminished in frequency. Stephanie felt miserable about not seeing her friend, but it had hurt too much for her to watch Marty being treated and, in her opinion, abused like that. She felt that she had no choice but to distance herself from the situation.

As she prepared for her inevitable confrontation with Roger, Marty let her mind wander to the day she had become friends with Stephanie.

. . .

It had been the Wednesday after Labor Day and the first day of school for most area students. The halls at Marion High School were bristling with the sights and sounds of book bags being hastily thrown into lockers and friends getting reacquainted after the long summer vacation. The seniors were exceptionally excited, knowing that they had become the new kings and queens of the hill. That was true, except for Marty. She was miserable and just wanted to get the year over with and move on to college.

With Peggy's death nearly three weeks prior still fresh in her mind, Marty had not fully prepared herself for the new school year: the onslaught of torment and ridicule she knew she was going to receive from her classmates. It was the same thing every year since coming to Marion, but she learned to deal with it. She had usually been able to block it out and go about her business. But that year had been different. She was too depressed and mentally unprepared to deal with anything the others were, inevitably, going to throw at her.

Marty Leonard opened her locker; the same old locker she had had for six years and neatly began to place her book bag, notebooks and folders into it. When finished, she took a deep breath. She adjusted her cranberry colored blouse and muttered, "Let's get this year over with." As she was shutting her locker door, she was startled by the presence of a girl from her class-- a girl she had not really cared for, nor respected: Stephanie Dawson.

"Hi, Marty," she said, nervously. "Can I talk to you a minute?"

Marty knew she was going to be picked on something

fierce, but she didn't think it would start so soon. This had been a new record. Expecting something nasty or even vulgar to come out of her mouth, Marty did not give Stephanie the satisfaction of an answer.

Stephanie Dawson was one of the girls who, in previous years, had been one of the main instigators. She had teased Marty, incessantly. Stephanie was pretty, having long, wavy, light brown hair that was usually pulled back into a ponytail. She also had a dark, glowing tan from the two weeks she spent in Florida, in late July.

Stephanie was wearing a blue and yellow tank top with a white, buttoned down, sleeveless shirt that didn't nearly have enough of them buttoned, in Marty's opinion. Although she didn't need any, she was also wearing blue eye shadow that had been put on a little too thick for Marty's taste. "At least the girl is color coordinated," she thought.

Unlike Stephanie, Marty would not resort to calling her anything even remotely questionable, even if she believed it to be true. Partly because she was beyond that sort of behavior and partly because she knew she was outnumbered and didn't want to start something she knew she wouldn't have been able to get herself out of. Being that she was the head cheerleader, Stephanie was popular. Marty had nicknamed all of the girls on the cheerleading squad the three "P's"; Pretty, Popular, and Preppy. She realized that it would have been all over for her if she had said anything derogatory towards Stephanie.

58

"Look, I know I haven't been very nice to you in the past, but can I just say something?" Stephanie said, almost pleading with her.

Marty, still somewhat leery of her, kept her guard up. She crossed her arms over her chest and said, "Okay, What would you like to talk about?"

An awkward silence fell between them for a few seconds, but, since she had already mustered enough courage to start the conversation, Stephanie decided to go for broke. "I just wanted to say that I heard about Peggy Thornton. I didn't know you were friends with her. My mom is friends with Mrs. T and she told me that you used to go over there a lot."

Marty looked down at her feet, choking back her tears and said, meekly, "We were close."

The first bell for homeroom sounded, giving them two minutes to finish their conversation.

"I know and I'm sorry. I'm sorry for a lot of things. I've misjudged you, Marty. I thought you had always felt that you were too good for us, but seeing that you were friends with Peggy got me to think that, maybe, we were wrong about you."

"Thanks. So, what are you saying?"

"I'm saying that I would like to be your friend, Marty, if you want. Look, I'm having a few friends over this weekend and I would like you to come, too."

Marty stared in disbelief. Had she heard this right? Was Stephanie asking her to come to a party? She was amazed and speechless.

"I realize that it is short notice, but I really would like you to come. Let me know if you can. Here's my phone number," she said, handing Marty a slip of paper.

Marty reached out and took it from her, still unable to say a word.

"Well, thanks for listening. I'll understand if you can't make it, but please try to come. It will be fun." Stephanie turned and briskly walked away, ponytail bobbing.

Marty stood, staring at the phone number Stephanie had given her. An eerie, but not unpleasant feeling came over her; a feeling as if Peggy, somehow, had something to do with this. Marty knew that that was impossible, yet that was exactly how she felt. Peggy told Marty that someday she would be pretty and have wings. Marty pictured Peggy as an angelic-like being, standing before God and interceding on her behalf. Marty looked up; not at the ceiling, but through it, and, giving a wink, said, "Thank you, Peggy. I guess you've earned your wings."

The second bell sounded, letting her know that she was, officially, late for homeroom. Smiling, she sprinted down the empty hallway to join the rest of her class.

That day, she remembered, was one of the best days of her high school career. She remembered going from class to class thinking about the exclusive party Stephanie was to be giving the following weekend. At first, she wondered whether or not it was a sick joke. She had read Stephen King's "Carrie" and, briefly, thought that those preppy girls might spring a trap and gang up on her. She analyzed every angle and found no holes in Stephanie's invitation. It was sincere. Marty believed it had taken a great deal of effort and courage, on Stephanie's part, to come to her locker and apologize. By the end of third period, Marty made up her mind to go to the party, but decided to wait until that evening to call her. She, also, decided to forgive everyone for all the callous, and, down right vicious things that had been said and done to her, in the past. She was willing to just let everything go.

From that day on, Stephanie and Marty were inseparable. Marty helped Stephanie with her attire and make-up and Stephanie helped Marty with her people skills. Stephanie could pour on the charm and talk to anyone. She could hold a conversation with anyone; even those whom she had only just met. Stephanie was far from shy. The other girls, however, hadn't been so benevolent and still didn't want much to do with her. Through the course of the year, they had no longer wanted to "hang out" with Stephanie, either. That had been all right with

61

Stephanie. She had matured. She wanted to be friends with someone who was "real"; a person with substance who wouldn't tell her what she had wanted to hear, but someone who wasn't afraid to tell her what she needed to hear. No matter how painful, Marty always told her the truth.

Early on in their friendship, Stephanie confided in Marty. Marty always gave good advice and seemed to know how best to handle any given situation. When she went to her with her dilemma, telling her that the other girls still didn't like her and had threatened not to be friends with her, either, Marty said, without batting an eye, "Do you really want to be friends with people like that, anyway?"

Stephanie thought about it, briefly. "Not no, but hell no."

Stephanie couldn't believe the answer was that simple. She had wrestled with it, for several days. No one had the right to intimidate another into doing something that that individual did not want to do and, certainly, not when it came down to a person who should be a friend. Mentally and physically, Stephanie Dawson was strong. Handling anything the others would want to throw at her, if they even dared, would not pose a problem. Let them threaten all they want. She had it covered. Stephanie liked Marty. She liked her for the individual she was and valued her friendship. If the others didn't want to climb on board, then she didn't need them.

By Christmas, teachers and family, alike, commented on

how Stephanie had changed. Her attire and make-up had become tasteful and more appropriate, bringing out her natural beauty. Even her attitude changed for the better. Yet, through it all, she was humble, giving credit to Marty for being instrumental in helping her create the person she had become.

Marty missed those high school days with Stephanie. Watching Stephanie grow into the refined woman she was, today, had been a highlight of her senior year. Marty took pleasure, and maybe, a touch of pride in knowing that she had played a major roll in the grooming process.

However, Marty was much better at giving advice than she was at receiving it. It was Stephanie who had told her not to marry Roger. Several times before the wedding, including the night before, Stephanie went to Marty, begging her not to wed the man. She thought Roger to be highly arrogant and had no use for his condescending remarks.

There was something else, too, that made Stephanie nervous, but it was not tangible. She could not place a finger on it. It was just this foreboding feeling she had whenever she was around him. She always felt that something bad was going to happen. The way he would look at her whenever Marty sided with him, on any given matter and the snide comments he would mutter under his breath would make her cringe and her blood boil. And, come to think of it, he always seemed to want to leave early when he saw that she and Marty were having a little too much fun, for his liking. It was as if he was trying to limit the time they could spend together. It was almost juvenile the way Roger conducted himself.

Marty didn't know everything that Stephanie had felt, but realized that when this ordeal was over, that is, if she survived it, she needed to call the best friend she ever had. She, also, vowed to call her mother. She hadn't heard from either one of them in months and, very well, knew why. She was feeling stupid and ashamed that she had let Roger come between her and the ones who cared about her the most. She was appalled at her own behavior. She allowed him to alienate her from her friends and family. Stephanie was like the sister she never had and it was her mother who, as she was growing up, pushed her into getting good grades. It was, now, her turn to apologize.

.   .   .

Marty took a bottle of extra-strength Tylenol out of the medicine cabinet and dry swallowed four of them. An incredibly chalky, bitter taste filled her mouth, as she hurried to get them down. The pain had subsided, somewhat, but she knew that it would flare up again once she tried to move. Then, she grabbed the medical tape and placed it on the edge of the vanity. Something caught her eye. Standing near the soap dish was a bottle of Windex. She did not remember putting it there. Next to it, she noticed a piece of paper toweling with a dark, crimson streak on the edge where it had been torn off from the rest of the sheet. Marty picked it up and studied it as if it were a science experiment gone awry. It looked like blood. In fact, she believed it to be her blood.

She scanned the room. Her vision was diminished because she could only see out of one eye, but she could see enough. No blood, anywhere, but on the rug where she had been; that and one of her missing teeth and a clump of her hair. Come to think of it, there was, also, a faint scent of bleach in the air. Roger must have been trying to clean up before he had left.

It made sense, but why had Roger taken the time to clean up? She asked herself. Maybe, she thought, he was trying to show her how sorry he was by taking the time to clean the mess. It was possible, but not probable. Roger didn't clean anything inside of the house, ever. There had to be another explanation. He would have realized that no amount of cleaning was going to save their marriage or prevent the law from coming after him. He wouldn't have bothered cleaning. Maybe, he didn't want the blood to dry on the walls, or, maybe, he thought he had already killed her and was trying to cover it up. The thought of that sent a shiver down her spine. Was that possible? Was Roger capable of that? Until seeing herself in the mirror, battered like she was, Marty would never have come to that conclusion. However, seeing the rage in his eyes and feeling how hard he had hit and kicked her, Marty believed that he was capable of anything, including murder.

She did not want to believe it, but there it was. She

couldn't un-think those thoughts. Could it be possible? Did he believe that he had already killed her? No. There had to be another, more rational, explanation for what had taken place. Why would he have left without trying to remove her and the rug? He couldn't possibly have meant to kill me, she rationalized. She tried to get the thought out of her mind, but could not. She was stunned and nervous. If I only knew where he was, she thought, I might have some insight as to what Roger was thinking. Marty forced herself to snap out of it. She still had a great deal of work to do.

Marty moved, gingerly, to the commode and lowered herself, slowly, down onto it, bracing herself against the pain. As she believed it would, it had come back with a vengeance. She held her leg out as straight as she could, as well as her breath, waiting for the pain to subside. The Tylenol had had little effect, but she was afraid to take any more. Once the pain decreased to where it had become bearable, she reached for the magazine rack next to the heat run that thankfully would not be needed for a couple months.

Spitefully, Marty took five of Rogers' "Hot Rod" and "Road and Track" magazines and set them on the floor next to her. Since he was the one who had broken her leg, she was going to use his magazines to splint it. The crutches used when she had sprained her ankle a few years back were in the downstairs bedroom closet. She was wishing, at the time, that they had been kept in the spare bedroom on the second floor.

66

Marty had desperately wanted to be a nurse practitioner. She spent hours reading medical books to learn different procedures and terminology, but Roger refused to let her go to college to pursue a career in medicine. However, that hadn't stopped Marty from learning on her own. Unfortunately, the little knowledge that she did have was needed to be put to good use on her own body.

Opening one of them until the binding started to crack Marty wrapped the magazine around her thigh and tightly secured it with long strips of medical tape from the roll she had retrieved from the cabinet. The next one she wrapped around her ankle and a third around her knee. Then, she used the other two to fill in the gaps, each time making sure they were tightly secured with tape. This provided her with the protection and stability she needed. She tried to bend her knee, but could not. It was completely immobile. That was the second item off her mental checklist. She looked at the clock on the wall. 2:37. Things were moving along, although much slower than she thought it should. Risking further injury, Marty felt that she was going to have to pick up the pace.

Roger had not arrived home, yet, and she was hoping for another hour, or so, before he did, in order to finalize her preparations. Marty wanted to be ready and have a fighting chance when he came home. She knew it was going to take some time in order to move into position downstairs. Where was Roger? Then, it came to her. She knew, exactly, where he might be. She remembered that it was Friday. He usually went down to

Rusty's Roost with the guys on Fridays. That further meant that he was not likely going to be home for a couple of hours. "But, why would he go there, knowing that I'm injured," she thought. He knew I was seriously injured. "He probably needed some time to cool off. Roger simply snapped. That's all there is to this," she said, aloud. "But, still, why would he do that?"

Marty did not want to believe that Roger had thought he had already killed her. She was emotionally devastated, but she believed there was nothing more to it than that. However, it did leave her with more questions than answers. The only way she was going to get them answered, she believed, was to confront him. At least, she thought she was going to have plenty of time to prepare for his return. Marty smiled inwardly to herself. The cards, she hoped, had started to turn in her favor.

Outside, the clouds were forming and an eerie calmness, one that, usually, warns of impending disaster, engulfed Marion.

Chapter IV

Roger's Plan

At about the time Marty was splinting her leg with the magazines, Matt asked Roger how his wife was. He was having a good time up until then and was not expecting the question. It came out of nowhere and he choked on the last swallow of beer he was drinking. He was coughing and gasping for breath.

"You okay, buddy?" Matt asked while patting him on the back.

"Yah. Just went down the wrong pipe, that's all."

Roger told Matt that he would be back in a minute, climbed down off of his bar stool and headed for the men's room. He actually just needed a few minutes to himself in order to regain his composure and figure out what he was going to do with Marty. He needed to plan a strategy on how he was going to dispose of the body and what he was going to say if someone had inquired about her, again. The way he saw it, it had been, relatively, easy to kill her. Getting rid of the evidence, on the other hand, was proving to be a much bigger task. He wished he had had more preparation time.

Standing in the larger, handicapped bathroom stall, Roger

focused on what he was going to tell the guys if they were to ask about Marty. Just telling them she was fine wasn't going to cut it. He needed something more; something believable.

Seconds were ticking away and nothing came to mind. He was becoming nervous and started pacing. Bankrupt of ideas, he was ready to give up, when he heard someone talking rather loudly in the bar about his sick mother. That's it, he thought. He would say that his wife was fine, but would be leaving that evening to visit her mother who, since Bill had passed away, had been living with her sister, in Binghamton. He was angry with himself for not being able to come up with that idea, sooner. It seemed so easy and believable. Marty hadn't seen her mother in over a year and it was far enough away to not make anyone think twice about it. It sounded credible to him, and shouldn't take much effort to sound convincing. Besides that, it would leave plenty of time to dispose of her body without arousing any suspicion. Confident that his thought would work, Roger decided to go ahead with the scenario.

The first, and least difficult, part of the problem had been solved, but the second, larger part, needed to be worked out. The major concern was what, indeed, to do with the body. He had not premeditated her murder, so he had not planned that far ahead. He felt bad for what he had done, but not bad enough to turn himself in. That was out of the question. Roger felt that he had worked too hard to see his dreams dashed against the rocks like a paddleboat in a hurricane. The thought of spending a good portion of his life in prison did not sit well, either. Tears of

70

frustration formed, as he came to grips with what he had done. In his mind, Marty did have something coming, make no mistake, but she didn't deserve to die.

That was not the entire reason for the sudden outburst of emotion, however. The main reason was that he was thinking about the humiliation his family, especially his mother, would endure if he was caught and convicted. The inquiries and lengthy trial would probably kill her. Then he would have two deaths he would be responsible for. His family did not deserve the repercussions stemming from any criminal action against him. He would, also, lose the farm that had been in the family for six generations. That would hurt more than anything else. He had put everything he had into it. Granted, he should have thought about all this before he had raised his hand against Marty, but it was, obviously, much too late for that. The only thing left to do was just what he was trying to do: take damage control measures. He had to insure that the crime was thoroughly, covered or, at least, disguised, so that he wouldn't be implicated in it. Roger felt that he could do that with proper planning. He never believed in luck.

Roger went back to focusing all of his attention on the question of what to do with Marty, who was, in his eyes, still lying dead on the bathroom floor. He considered burying the body on the hill, in the woods behind the house, but quickly determined that the cadaver dogs would be able to find her, easily, and scratched the thought, entirely. Reprimanding himself for coming up with such a stupid thought, Roger said aloud,

"You idiot. Think of something better than that or you'll be in jail before the day is over."

Roger realized that it was not a good idea to hide the body anywhere on the property. The pond wasn't deep enough and the fields were too risky. He was going to have to take it somewhere, but where? Other questions arose. How was he going to transport it and, just as important, how was he going to get back once he had disposed of it? This was becoming far too complicated for his liking.

As he tried to work out the details, Roger went to the sink to wash his hands. He splashed cold water on his face. The situation was unnerving and causing him a great deal of fatigue. Wishing he had some extra-strength Tylenol, Roger ran his wet fingers through his hair. He had a splitting headache.

Granted, he had bought himself some time by knowing what he was going to say if anyone asked how Marty was. He could worry about the other details, later. It's just that he wanted to have a specific plan—for his own sanity. He didn't like loose ends, in this case. Things could, easily, get out of hand. His life was on the line and he knew it. But Roger had been in the men's room for quite some time and he believed that Matt would soon be in to see if he was all right. Maybe, he would be given a couple more minutes to work out the details.

Trying to stay focused, Roger was determined to work on his predicament. At first, the answer eluded him, but it occurred to him that he had better start with a mental inventory of the things he was going to need to accomplish his horrific duty. He began with a list of the vehicles he had at his disposal. Since he was going to have to transport the body, he needed to know which one he was going to use. He had the pick-up, Marty's Buick wagon that she had used when grocery shopping, an ATV, and the farm equipment. None of the farm equipment struck him as being suitable, but he listed them anyway. He might need a tarp to conceal the body and some old clothes and shoes, as well. He would need something to wear that he wouldn't miss and could be burned, easily. Because the story had been to say that Marty was away visiting her mother, he was also going to need a couple of suit cases to pack a week worth of clothes, to make it look realistic and believable.

As Roger began to form this part of the plan, another problem arose. It seemed like the more questions he answered the more that needed to be answered. If he dumped the body along the side of the road and drove back, he was taking a chance that the authorities would find blood or other evidence, in the vehicle, linking him to the crime. Besides, Marty was supposed to be visiting her mother. What was he going to say to that? How could his wife's body be found miles away from home, when she was supposed to be driving to visit her mother, and yet all of the vehicles registered to Roger were still accounted for? That would not be good. Yet, if he left the vehicle at the scene, how did he intend on getting back?

Roger began to see a wider scope of problems. He

believed that there was, absolutely, no way that he was going to be able to drive the same vehicle home without drawing red flags from the investigators. It would be much too risky. He ran the other scenario in his mind. If he was forced to leave a vehicle behind, the use of his truck was out of the question. Roger was not about to leave his precious Silverado at the scene. But, if he used the wagon, he may not even have to wrap the body; just set it in the car after having cleaned it up. He would not even have to wear gloves during transport, because it would seem logical that his fingerprints would be on a vehicle that he had owned. It would, definitely, look like foul play, but not necessarily link him to the crime. Since he had just fueled the wagon up the day before, it would have nearly a full tank of gas. Roger had made up his mind. He would leave the wagon at the scene. The only problem remaining was how he planned on getting back. Just then, the door opened.

"Hey, Rog. You still in here, buddy? You didn't fall in, did you?" It was Matt with more than just a slight tone of concern.

"Yah, I'm in here. I'm just not feeling very well, that's all." That was no lie.

"You had me worried there. Is everything okay? You didn't look to good when you left the bar. I thought I would come and check in on you."

"I said I'm all right."

74

The annoyed tone in his voice was unmistakable.

Matt was taken by surprise. He had heard Roger talk disrespectfully to others, but never to him. "All right. No need to get upset. I just thought you might be having some problems and needed some help, that's all.".

"If I needed any help, I would've called," Roger stated, sarcastically.

"I came in here thinking something might be wrong. Sorry if I was so concerned," Matt stated, crossly. "Anyway, your food is getting cold." He turned, disgusted with Roger's behavior and returned to the bar.

Roger heard the door shut behind him. He was frustrated, but tried to regain his thoughts and composure and settled back to work on his predicament. He had been in the bathroom for nearly 20 minutes and the longer he stayed, the more nervous and upset he was becoming.

Roger hated to be interrupted when he was working on something. He thought about calling it a day and taking his lunch to go when he heard the sound of a motorcycle pulling in. Wait a minute, he thought to himself-- a gleam in his eye. He had an old Yamaha 150 dirt bike from when he was a kid, in the barn. The last time he had been on it was two summers previous when the ATV broke down. He had forgotten all about it. "All I would need to do," he thought, "is change the spark plugs and put fresh gas in it and it should be good to go." That was it. It could work.

In his mind, Roger had most of the details figured out. With the main pieces to the puzzle in place the others started falling, as well. Ideas came so fast that his mind had a hard time keeping up. He would take the wagon to the barn, after dark, and load the dirt bike into the back, then, back the wagon up to the house. Everything inside would be cleaned up by then. He would place the body into the back seat, along with the two suitcases. He would drive toward Binghamton, taking the back roads to routes 5 and 20, instead of the thruway. It would be less traveled and he would be able to avoid the tollbooths. No sense taking any chances on someone remembering him. He would then drive for thirty or forty miles and look for a quiet dumping spot. Then he would push the body out of the car, making it look like Marty had an altercation.

Carefully, he would take the dirt bike out from the back and drive home leaving the rest behind. Of course he would have to get rid of the shoes he was wearing at the scene and put on a different pair, so that the prints wouldn't match. In fact, he thought, he should wear a larger sized pair in order to throw off the investigators. The farm hands always left boots lying around the barn. He could just take one of theirs. Roger would also have to cover any tire marks left by the dirt bike and make sure that no trace of it could be found. The details to Rogers' plan were, finally, finished and he was fairly confident that it was going to work.

76

Relieved, Roger splashed more water on his face and rubbed his neck. The stress had caused him to become hot and sweaty and his headache had greatly intensified. In more ways than one, Roger had become a ticking time bomb.

Gazing into the mirror, Roger, apparently not particularly caring for the reflection looking back at him, lowered his head. He was unable to look at himself. A minute prior, he was thinking how well he had worked out the problem about what to do with the body, even though he had been interrupted. But, he was back to feeling confused. His muscles tensed. Various emotions jockeyed for position inside his head. He was ashamed at the person he was becoming, and angry at the "created" circumstances. Pleased with the way he had solved the problems, while feeling miserable for having committed this awful crime. Nothing made sense. He wanted, desperately, to turn the clock back a couple of hours. Another tear formed out of frustration. It rolled down his cheek, stopping at the corner of his mouth. Feeling the salty wetness upon his tongue, Roger had not only tasted the bitterness of his tears, but, possibly the bitter consequences of his actions, as well.

In just a few short hours, Roger's world had collapsed. There were choices he had to make and he, clearly, did not make the right ones. As a result, things had gotten out of hand. One thing he knew for sure; he needed an ally and thought it best to go back into the bar and apologize to Matt. Not because he had wanted to or because he felt that he had been wrong, but because, he felt, he had to. Roger never apologized to anyone, thinking it beneath him to do so. Why should he? He was always right. It was just that he did not want to draw any negative attention to himself and felt that it was the only, logical, thing to do. He was dwelling on things that he no longer had any control over and was wallowing in self-pity. Looking in the mirror at his own reflection, he said aloud "Stop your incessant whining and be a man." He left the restroom, shaking his head, and returned to his friend at the bar, leaving the door wide open.

Walking past the pinball machines and pool table, Roger went back to the bar and found his seat. His lunch, like Matt had said, was sitting on the counter, waiting for him. Unlike in most restaurants, it looked as good on the plate as it did in the picture on the menu. Standing along side it, at attention, was a full bottle of Heinz ketchup. Jean truly did make the best tasting cheeseburgers around. Matt was already three-quarters finished with his wings, the sauce sticking to his fingers, when Roger strolled up.

Roger took the bun off of the burger, placed it on the onion rings, and picked up the bottle of ketchup. He glanced in Matt's direction and, almost sounding sincere, said, "I'm sorry I talked to you like that, man. I'm just not feeling very well."

"Having a bad day?" he asked, licking his fingers.

"You do not know the half of it." That was no lie.

"We all have bad days, sometimes. Besides, I know you

were having a choking spell before you got up and left. Don't sweat the small stuff." Matt was amazed that Roger had apologized to him, but didn't want to show he was.

Pouring ketchup onto the burger, Roger said, "I know, but I shouldn't have exploded like that. You were only concerned and I shouldn't have spoken to you like that. You didn't deserve it and I'm sorry."

Roger took a bite of his burger; juice dripping down his chin. He picked up a napkin and wiped it off.

Matt had been staring at Roger in disbelief. He never expected him to apologize the first time, but twice, that was unheard of. "It's okay, Rog."

Matt picked up another wing and dabbed it in hot sauce before biting into it. He was still in shock over Rogers' change of heart. Maybe, he thought, Roger is trying to change his ways. Yet, in the back of his mind, Matt knew his track record. It would take a lot more than just this one apology to convince him that Roger was trying to become a better person. For now, the jury was still out.

While they ate their lunch, Matt and Roger occupied the time with small talk: how it looked like Torre and the Yankees were going to make the post-season, yet again; that, unless something drastic happened, the area farmers were sure to have a good crop, this year; and the possibility of a severe thunderstorm, later in the day. If they had looked outside, they would have seen the thickening clouds forming high in the western sky, warning of one coming.

Just as they were finishing up the last of their lunch, a question was asked, behind them, which was like music to Matt's ears. "You boys sticking around for a little nine ball, today." That could only be one man. Turning in the direction the voice had come from, they saw Eric White and Karl Pearson, each with a pool cue in hand and each with the same, mischievous smile. Eric was tall and slender, in his late thirties, with a full head of wavy light brown hair and a thick handlebar mustache. He worked for the Monroe County Airport, on the west side of the city, fueling aircraft. Karl was a biology teacher at the Marion High School. He liked his students and enjoyed teaching, but he liked the summer vacations more. Including the top of his head, because he did not want anyone to realize that he was starting to go bald, Karl was clean shaven. He was forty-one, but you couldn't tell by looking at him. He worked out daily and ran three times a week, religiously.

They were both pretty fair pool players, each able to run a table, but Matt and Roger could hold their own, at times. Roger was the least proficient of the four, but had been known to get hot on occasion.

"If you guys are up to getting your butts whipped, Eric," Matt said, smiling.

"Oh, no. It's gonna be just like last week, Matt. We beat you guys three-to-two," Karl pointed out as he went over to shake his hand. "You guys are gonna get spanked."

"Care for the same friendly wager, gentlemen? Roger's due for a couple of good games. You're going to be buying the rounds, this time."

"Sure. But I think you are quite mistaken, Mr. Tillman." Eric said, with a fair imitation of a British accent. "I can taste those free, zero denarii, at no cost to myself, cold ones, already."

"You feelin' up to it, Rog?" Karl asked, luring him into the conversation.

Roger, who had wanted to get back home for obvious reasons, said, "I don't know guys." I should be getting home in a bit."

"Come on, Rog. Just one or two games," Matt pleaded.

"Yah. Come on, Rog. We're looking forward to a little butt whuppin'. That's yours, by the way," Karl said, jesting.

Roger, being the competitor that he was and never backing down from a challenge, stated, "All right, since you put it that way, I'm up for a few. Rack 'em boys."

Matt told Rusty that he was buying a round of beers for the guys and a couple of minutes later, came into the game room with two open bottles of Coors in each hand.

Rusty reminded them, more for Rogers' ears than the others, "No drinks on the pool table, gentlemen."

They answered with, "No problem, Rusty." "Ok, boss." And "Yes sir, Rus." That is, except Roger. He never said a word.

Roger actually played well the first game and he and Matt wound up taking it. But things fell apart, after that. Roger was more concerned with matters at home to be able to concentrate on his shots. Once in the third game, the nine ball Roger had taken aim at caromed wildly off of a corner pocket. It would have given them a nice two game to one edge. Instead, Eric made the easy shot into the side pocket giving his team the lead, which they never relinquished. This had made Roger visibly angry. He never recovered his composure. By the end of the fourth game, Roger was throwing his pool stick and swearing, prompting Rusty to look in and tell him to keep it down.

Matt was clearly upset with Rogers' behavior, while Eric and Karl were, totally, amused by his antics. They did not care how loud he got. It seemed like the angrier he became, the worse he played.

After the fifth game, Matt had had enough. They had lost four out of five to Eric and Karl, but he was not disappointed in

82

the way the pair had played. For the most part, they were good sports about it and had not rubbed it in. It was Roger whom he had been angry with and not because of the way he had played, either. Roger hadn't played that poorly. He just missed the shots that counted most. It was Rogers' juvenile-like tantrums that made him upset. Roger could be a jerk, at times, but his behavior, that day, had been worse than he had ever seen. He went above and beyond being his usual idiot self. Something, Matt thought, is bothering him. But, whatever the reason was, he realized that Roger was, simply, never going to change and that troubled him. He enjoyed Rogers' company when he was acting in a more civilized manner, but he never knew when he was going to get fired up about something. Matt was getting too old for the nonsense.

"Well, gentlemen," Eric stated, with the same British accent as earlier, "I guess you owe us four beers, but because you guys bought the first round, we'll make it only three."

Matt, willingly, took out a ten and handed it to Karl, while Roger, hastily took out two fives and, grudgingly, slammed them on the pool table and stormed out of the room without saying a word.

Eric, picking them up, said, "Pleasure doing business with you, boys. Those cold ones are going to taste mighty fine."

"Hope you guys had fun. Sorry for the outburst," Matt said, trying to apologize for Rogers' actions, as he pointed to the door Roger had just exited.

But, Eric, realizing the source, said matter-of-factly "Don't sweat it, boss."

"Yah, it's okay, Matt. We understand," Karl added, although he honestly couldn't.

"Well, I guess I had better get out there and see what 'ol Rog is doing. See you guys next week."

.   .   .

Back inside the bar area, Roger was nursing his fourth and last nerve calming brew before calling it a day. It was ten after four and he had been in Rusty's a great deal longer than he wanted to. He just needed this last one to get his head on straight. Outside, the storm, gaining strength by the minute, just blocked the rays of the late afternoon sun.

Matt sat down next to Roger, shaking his head. "What's gotten into you, Rog?"

Turning, he bellowed, "I'm sorry, okay?"

"I'm just trying to help. If something is bothering you, don't keep it bottled up inside you. I know things haven't gone

84

very well for you in the past, so talk to me about it. Maybe I can help."

"If I wanted your help, I would have asked for it, Dr. Phil."

"What is wrong with you, man?"

"Nothin.' Leave me alone."

The two of them stared at each other in awkward silence. Finally, after seeing that Roger was not going to budge, Matt broke it. "Fine. If you don't want to talk, I'm outa here. Rusty, I'll see you, later. Have a nice day," he said, waving a hand.

"Take care, Matt. Hey, be careful driving. Looks like a bad storm is on the way, at least that's what I just read on the news flash."

"Thanks. I'll be okay," he said, giving one last disgusted look at Roger before exiting out the front door.

Roger never said good-bye to him. He just kept staring at his beer bottle as he drained the last of it.

It was the last time Roger ever saw him.

Walking up to Roger from behind the bar, Rusty said, "Ya know, Rog. You should be nicer to your friend, Matt. You don't have too many left in this world."

"What do you know, old man?" he snapped, getting up to leave.

The phone rang just as Rusty was about to tell him just what he knew, saving Roger from further embarrassment. Roger, starting to walk across the room for the exit, heard him say, "Yah, he's still hear. You want to talk to him? Sure."

Rusty thought, for a split second, about letting Roger walk out of his bar without saying a word to stop him, telling Marty that he wasn't able to catch him before he had walked out. Actually, he was glad to be rid of him. It's just that he was more than curious as to what Marty wanted. Not only had she rarely ever called her husband there, she also did not sound like herself. He had a gut feeling that something was wrong. He thought he would hang around and listen in on the conversation. As much as Rusty had hated to call Roger back to the bar, he felt compelled to do so.

Just as Roger reached the exit, Rusty, quickly, yelled to him. "Roger, telephone. It's your wife."

Chapter V

Call to Steph

Marty was in a seated position on the bathroom floor, with her legs out in front of her. The makeshift splint she had made for her leg with Rogers' magazines, had been working like a charm; much better than she ever expected. Even after she bumped it while lowering herself from the commode, Marty had not experienced much pain. However, she was forced to use her arms to propel herself along the floor a great deal more than she wanted to. She didn't have a choice. It was her only mode of transportation. She knew that she would not have been able to hop on one foot that great a distance. Besides, if one was already on the floor, she rationalized, one could not fall. Unfortunately, it caused her increasing discomfort in her chest with each pendulum swing of her arms; however, Marty was on a mission and completely focused.

Yet, knowing that Roger, in all likelihood, would be home within a couple of hours motivated her to continue at a fast pace. She slid her way across the room, down the long hallway, and positioned herself at the top of the stairs. Marty knew that there was still a great deal of work to be done, before she would feel confident enough to confront him. Yet, all things considered, Marty was starting to feel a little better about her situation; that was, until she had made it to the stairs.

Looking down the long flight of stairs, Marty realized what an obstacle it posed for someone in her condition. Her chest was throbbing, already, and she knew the stairs were going to be harder to navigate. She was going to have to rest before attempting to head down. It was either that, or remain seated at the top of the landing for Roger to come home. That was out of the question. After a few minutes, the throbbing in her ribs let up enough for her to start her descent. Carefully, she lowered herself down the first of the fifteen steps, keeping her injured leg out in front of her and guarding her broken ribs as best she could.

Each step, as she continued her descent, caused further difficulty and increased pain. She could both hear and feel the crepitus of her shattered ribs with every movement. The pendulum-like motion allowed the jagged edges to cut into her flesh, similar to the action of a handsaw cutting wood. Her chest felt as if it were on fire. The stabbing, burning sensation became unbearable and tears began to well up in her eyes. She grunted, in anger, trying to will them away.

Four steps from the bottom, Marty was no longer able to bear the pain and was forced to stop and rest her aching body. She was having trouble concentrating and her thoughts became scrambled. Brightly colored stars filled her vision and she started to lose her sense of balance. Marty was on the verge of passing out. "If that happens," she thought, "I'll tumble the rest of the way down and kill myself." Marty did the only thing she could think of: close her eye and shake her head from side to side. She let out a controlled scream.

It worked. The dizzy feeling slowly dissipated. At last, she opened her eye. The spots were gone. That had been a close one. She chastised herself for pushing too hard. Yet, on the other hand, she knew that time was getting short. It was an altogether unnerving situation; the ultimate "Catch Twenty-Two." How was she going to balance her sense of urgency with the need to be prudent? She didn't like being forced into this position. She didn't like it at all.

Marty continued her descent; this time at a slower pace. She had to face the fact that she was just going to have to take it a little easy and hope she was in a position to defend herself when Roger came home. When she finally reached the last step, she leaned forward until she was able to look out of the living room window, to the driveway. No truck, yet. Good.

Marty opted to continue across the living room as she had been and not try to stand. She didn't think that she could prevent herself from passing out from overexertion. Continue with what works. "At least," she thought, "I have made it this far, and with any luck, I'll make it the rest of the way."

Halfway across the room, past the two solid oak bookcases that had become her life over the years, Marty spotted the cordless telephone sitting on the end table, near the LAY-Z-BOY recliner. It was still in its cradle. She froze, momentarily. This could be her lifeline, her salvation. With a renewed sense of urgency, Marty quickened her pace. The pain was still there, but it no longer seemed to matter. Upon reaching it, Marty picked up the receiver and placed it to her ear. A dial tone. "Thank God," she whispered. Roger did not unplug it. She would not have been able to plug it back in, being that the jack was behind the chair. She wouldn't have been able to move it.

Holding it for too long without dialing, the receiver started to make that peculiar, but distinct, warbling sound; letting her know to hang up and try again. She did so, immediately intending to dial 911 just as her mother did on the day her father died. As she started to push the second number, again, she froze. This time, because she hadn't fully thought out the consequences of her action.

"What would likely happen if I do call the police," she thought? Being that it was a domestic dispute with injuries, Marty surmised that the police would get to the house, rather quickly, followed by an ambulance. She would be taken to the hospital. Once Roger had finally arrived home, he would be taken into custody for the brutal attack and arrested. No confronting Roger on her own terms. No watching him being led away in handcuffs. In all likelihood, she wouldn't be able to even make a statement until she came out of surgery. Not acceptable.

Marty wanted to confront Roger on her terms for only one reason. It wasn't so much to find out why he had beaten her so badly, although she did want to know that. More importantly, it was to tell him she was taking her life back and that he would be powerless to stop her from doing so. She wanted to show him that she was, no longer, going to be intimidated by him. By calling the men and women in blue, she understood that she was not going to get that opportunity. It would be out of her hands. Again, not acceptable.

The receiver started making that incessant warbling noise for the second time in as many minutes and she hung it back up. Marty stared at it, wondering what she should do. If Roger came home this very minute, she would have no choice but to call the police. But, she felt that she still had enough time to be able to do this her way.

She had a need to tell someone, but she also needed to be able to trust that the person she called would not contact the authorities. Any agency, such as lifeline or a woman's shelter, would be obligated to contact them. Her mother, she knew, would, most certainly, call. Stephanie? It had been such a long time since she talked to her, ten months, not counting the class reunion, in June. Marty had promised to call her, but Roger made that difficult. Would Stephanie even want to talk to her? Even if she did, Marty knew how she felt about Roger. She had never kept that a secret. Could she be trusted to keep it to herself, at least until Marty had time to do what she felt she needed to do? There was only one way to find out. Reluctantly, she picked up the receiver, again, and dialed Stephanie's number.

Stephanie was not the domestic type, but rather, a free spirit, so Marty wondered if the woman was even at home. The phone rang three times at the other end and she had, already, become discouraged. Please, be home, she thought. After the amount of rings had doubled, she believed that Stephanie was out and gave up. Almost in tears, she, slowly, lowered the phone from her ear. As the receiver was about to reach its cradle, Marty could hear a faint, winded "Hello". Marty tried to bring it back up to her ear, but dropped it. She picked it back up, again and heard a second, exasperated "Hello" before Marty had the chance to acknowledge the first one.

"Hi, Steph."

"Marty, is that you? You're the only one who still calls me Steph."

"Yes. It's me."

"I don't mean to sound cruel, but you sound terrible. Is everything all right?"

Marty hadn't given it a thought. She hadn't said very much since reviving on the bathroom floor nearly an hour and a half previous. Without her upper two front teeth, along with the added fat lip, she was speaking with a noticeable lisp.

"No. Not good at all."

"I see. What did he do to you?" she asked, intuitively. She knew Roger had something to do with it.

92

"I don't have much time. I need you to listen to me. You got a minute?"

"Yah, sure, Marty. What did he do to you? Stephanie pressed.

"I'm going to tell you, everything. You're the only one I can trust."

Marty told her everything she could remember about the events that had taken place that afternoon. She could hear Stephanie crying on the other end, as she described her ordeal; the broken bones, the excruciating pain she had been experiencing, and how she splinted her leg. She even remembered to tell her about finding the bottle of Windex, on the vanity.

"That moron was trying to clean up the mess," Stephanie interjected.

"That's what I thought, too."

"Where is that son-of-a...?"

"Probably down at Rusty's Roost," she said, interrupting Stephanie.

"I'm coming over. Be there in..."

"NO! You can't. Please don't. I don't want you to get involved any more than you already are."

"Why, Marty. Can't you see he tried to kill you?" Stephanie pleaded.

"I'm not so sure that he was trying to kill me, but, either way, I am going to leave him. I need to confront him on my terms, though. That's why I haven't called for an ambulance or gotten the police involved."

"Marty, this is insane. I can't let you do this."

"Please, listen to me. You have been my best friend for a long time. Except for the reunion, we haven't seen much of each other because of Roger. I take that back; I allowed Roger to control me. That's going to change, as of today," she said, fighting back the tears. "I'm sorry for everything, Steph. You have to believe me and you have to promise me that you won't call the police."

"I can't do that. You're asking me to keep silent knowing that it could get you killed. No. I'm not okay with that."

"Promise me. I have got to do this on my own. I got myself into this mess, I must try to get myself out of it."

"Marty, you are in no shape to confront... HIM."

"I know. But, I have a plan."

"Whatever it is, it isn't going to work."

"Stephanie, promise me."

"Marty, I..."

"Promise me," Marty interrupted, again.

An awkward silence fell between them. Marty could hear the faint crackle in the receiver, allowing her to know that they were still connected. After nearly half a minute, Marty thought that she might be mistaken about the connection and said, "Hello."

"I'm still here, Marty, I was just thinking, that's all. So, tell me about this plan of yours."

Marty told her that it had not been her intent to face Roger without protection. If time permitted, she would load the rifle that Roger kept in the bedroom closet, place it in the living room window and, like a soldier in a foxhole, wait for him to come home. As soon as she saw his truck coming down the road, she would dial 911 and tell the dispatcher that she needed the police and an ambulance; that she had been severely beaten by her husband. Marty also stated that she would only allow him as far as the walkway, keeping him locked out with the weapon pointed at him at all times. Then, she would tell him that she would be pressing charges against him and filing for divorce.

"Marty, I can't believe you're going to bring a gun into the picture. What if he comes home before you can load it? What if he takes the gun away from you?"

"If Roger comes home before I have the chance to load the rifle, I'll call the police immediately, but, I assure you, he isn't going to be able to take it from me."

"There are a lot of- 'What-ifs.' What if he continues toward the house after you tell him to stop and you wind up shooting him? Or, worse. What if you miss or just can't pull the trigger? He'll kill you, Marty. He would realize he has lost everything. There would be nothing left to lose. Heck, even the recoil could kill you"

"You have valid points. They are all good and you may be right, but I have got to do this, Steph: for me. Besides, the cops will be here before anything can happen."

"This is crazy. I'm so worried about you."

"I can't say that I'm not worried, myself."

"Then, for God's sake, why do you want to do something like this and why are you telling me?"

"For a better part of the last 15 years, even before we got

married, Roger has told me what to do: how to cook, how to clean, the friends I could have and how long I could see them. He has controlled nearly every aspect of my life through intimidation, through mental and physical abuse. NO MORE! I'm tired of the mind-games. I'm taking my life back. If I call the police, now, I won't be given the opportunity to confront him. Somebody else will be giving me my life back. I need to take it back my own way. I want you to know because you are my best friend and I trust you. In case something does go wrong, I need you to know why I am doing this."

Stephanie was silent, once again, on the other end of the line. She knew that Marty had made up her mind and that she wasn't going to change it. She could see her point, but saw the dangers, as well. She only had two options. To either honor the wishes of her long time friend by not saying anything to the police, or calling them and risk the destruction of her friendship with Marty. Stephanie was torn: torn between what she knew she should do and what her best friend had asked her to do.

"Okay, Marty. I see your point," she said, finally. "I won't say anything, but I still don't like this. Too many things can go wrong. I'm having a hard time leaving you, like this. You have broken bones, deep cuts and God knows what else and you're asking me to take a business-as-usual approach. You're in no shape to do this" She had to try to make Marty see reason one last time.

"He probably feels bad about what he has done to me,

now that he's cooled off. He will try to apologize. I don't think he intentionally tried to kill me. Roger snapped; that's all. I'm just never going to give him the opportunity to beat me like that ever again. This will be the last time any man ever lays a hand on me."

"I tried to warn you about him along time ago, Marty."

"I know. Everyone did, including my parents. I just, obviously, didn't see or didn't want to see, what others saw in him," Marty admitted.

"Will you promise me something, since I promised you I wouldn't say anything to anyone?"

Tentatively, Marty agreed. "I guess I owe you that much."

"Just promise me that you'll call me if something else goes wrong; if you further injure yourself."

"I have you on speed-dial, Steph, but if something happens, I doubt if there'll be any t..."

"Okay, I get the point, Marty," Stephanie interrupted. "You should have married Zach Sharrow. He really loved you; still does." There. After all these years, Stephanie finally told her how she felt about her choice of men.

It

was Marty's turn to, upon hearing the name, fall silent. She remembered being torn between Roger and Zach the summer after graduation. It was only because Zach had decided to pursue an engineering degree at the Massachusetts Institute of Technology that Marty decided to stop seeing him. Marty wanted to stay closer to home, opting to go to Nazareth. She never got the opportunity, anyway. Roger insisted she stay in Marion after high school to build their relationship; that she could always go, later. Marty fell for it. Even then, Roger wanted total control of her life.

Her parents had been furious with the both of them. Julia counseled her daughter, telling her that once she decided to wait a few years to continue her education it would be extremely difficult for her to go back to school, especially if she started a family. Bill took a different approach. He was angry at his daughter for throwing away the scholarships she had earned. He moped around the house for weeks after she told him that she was going to stay in Marion and cultivate her relationship with Roger. But, as angry as he was with her, she knew, in the end, that she would always be his little girl and could not stay mad at her. Sure, enough, six weeks later, Bill sat down with his daughter and had a heart-to-heart talk with her, finishing their conversation with a long, warm, fatherly hug that let her know that he still loved her and always would.

"Where did that come from?" Marty finally asked.

"He still likes you, y'know."

Uncomfortable talking about this, just yet, Marty said, "I better go, Steph. I have so much to do before Roger gets home. Thanks for listening. Have a good day."

"I was until about ten minutes ago."

"I know and I'm sorry."

"It's okay. I'm the one who should be sorry. I can't believe I'm just going to hang up this phone and not do anything."

"Thanks, Steph. You're one in a million. See ya later. Kiss the kids for me."

Marty hung up the phone and looked into the kitchen to see what time it was. From her position, she could see the rooster clock on the wall, above the sink. 3:32. Time was going by quickly and she still had a few things left to prepare. The clouds, continuing to increase in both size and strength, were darkening the western sky. It wouldn't be long before they blocked the suns rays. And it wouldn't be long before the little burg of Marion would feel the full blow from Mother Nature's fury.

As she slowly moved across the floor, making her way into the bedroom, Marty's thoughts drifted to the summer that seemed so long ago to think about the man Stephanie had told her she should have married.

Chapter VI

Prom Night

Zachary Sharrow was an intelligent, reserved young man with a bright future ahead of him. Standing six-four, and weighing 235, along with the hours he spent in the weight room each week had made him menacingly big. Others would stand aside and let the big guy pass when he walked through a class or lunch line. He wasn't mean, but no one knew differently, because he was so quiet. Zach didn't have a great deal to say about anything. What he did have was chiseled features; short, cropped, sandy-blond hair kept in a neat, military-like flattop with matching full beard, and piercing, cobalt blue eyes. Because he was one of the few young men in school with a full beard, Zachary had always been mistaken for someone who was much older.

The only sources of entertainment for the young Mr. Sharrow, other than the weight room, had been books and basketball. They had been, pretty much, the only things that had interested him. Much of his self-allowed free time was spent honing his skills on the court. He spent countless hours, in the off-season at the community center in Lyons trying to improve his shot percentage. Zachary was not the best player on the team, but on defense, he was unbelievable. Almost nothing got past the big man. For the most part, however, if he wasn't in the gym or on the court, Zach Sharrow was in a book. History, bridge construction, thermonuclear reactors-- just about anything caught his interest. He learned new concepts quickly and learned them well, memorizing many difficult formulas in calculus and physics.

Unlike others who saw Zach's quietness as being standoffish or even intimidating, Marty, possibly because she had been misunderstood as well, thought him to be shy and quite likeable. Her observation was that he didn't have the time for much of anything, including friends. He seemed diligent in his studies, kept quietly to himself, and didn't have the patience for the trivial conversations of the average teen. Zach tolerated stupidity even less. She liked that about him. She liked the fact that he would walk away from the typical high school drama of the other students and respected him for his intelligence.

Two weeks before the prom, Zachary, ever the shy one was able to muster enough courage to ask Marty to the big dance. Well, at least he had gained enough courage to ask Stephanie if she would, in turn, ask Marty if she would go with him to the prom. He gave her his number to give to Marty and hoped for the best. Stephanie was more than delighted. She had been even more excited to ask Marty than he was. She couldn't wait to see Marty at lunch to tell her the good news.

At 11:40, Stephanie Dawson ran up to Marty carrying her economics book in one hand and a small, plastic bag with her lunch, neatly tucked away inside, in the other.

"Somebody likes you, Marty," she teased.

"Oh yah, who?" Marty answered. She would not have believed a word of it had it been said by anyone else.

"Zach Sharrow."

They sat down at a small, empty round table towards the back of the cafeteria, away from the others.

"Zach Sharrow. You're kidding," Marty said, placing her books in the empty seat next to her and setting her lunch on the table in front of her.

"Nope. He asked me if you were going to the prom with anyone. I told him a lie and said I didn't know, but that I would find out."

"Really? He wants to take me to the dance?"

"Would I lie to you? Don't answer that. Anyway, he said that he would like to take you if you weren't going with someone else."

"I'm not, I mean, I would, I mean, yes," Marty stuttered excitedly.

"Well, tell him," Stephanie said, as she took a spoon, a container of yogurt, and a banana out of her lunch bag.

"I don't know what to say. No one has ever asked me out before. I don't even have a prom dress."

"First things, first. You have to tell Zach that you intend to go. We'll worry about the dress, later." Then, she added, "You are really new at this."

Marty lowered her head in shame.

"It's ok, Marty. No need to feel embarrassed. You're going to look beautiful."

Marty knew that Stephanie had gone out with several guys in school and she had felt a little out of place. She didn't really know what to say.

"So, what do you think of him?" Stephanie asked, giving Marty a playful wink.

"Zach is nice, but he's so quiet."

"Yah, but he's smart, like you."

"That's true," Marty said, not out of arrogance or conceit, but only to acknowledge that she and Zach had something in common.

"My, aren't we conceited."

"I didn't mean it like that."

"I know. I just wanted to give you a hard time. Well, just give him call him. Here, he gave me his number to give to you." She handed Marty a slip of paper similar to the one she had handed to her at the beginning of the school year with her own number on it. "Aren't you gonna eat your lunch?" she added, giving a slight nod towards the bag that Marty had set aside.

"Suddenly, I no longer feel hungry, Steph. I'm too excited to eat."

"Well, I can't blame you. So, then, can I have your chips? This health food is killing me."

Marty laughed, handing the bag to Stephanie. "Sure, go ahead."

.   .   .

Later that evening, Marty decided that she had made Zachary wait long enough and dialed his number. He must have been anxiously waiting by the phone, because she didn't even hear it ring on her end before it had been picked up.

"H-Hello," Zachary said, nervously.

" Hello. Is Zach there, please? This is Marty Leonard."

"This is Zach. Hi, Marty. I was hoping that you would call me."

"I think I've only talked to you, a couple of times. I didn't remember what your voice sounded like. Stephanie told me that you wanted to ask me something. What's up?" she said, not letting on that she already knew what it was about.

"She didn't tell you?"

"No." Marty heard a deep sigh on the other end, followed by a moment of silence. She held the phone away from her face so that he wouldn't hear her laughing. She was enjoying making him feel uncomfortable.

"I, ah, just wanted to know if you had a date for the prom, that's all," he blurted out, relieved that the, almost, question was finally out.

Marty was thrilled. It had been the first time that anyone of the opposite sex had ever asked her to go anywhere. "Are you asking me if I would go with you?"

"Yes, Marty, I guess I am." His confidence level was only slightly higher, since his previous statement. But, since the question had been asked, the worse thing that could happen,

106

although he surely didn't want it to, would be if she had said, "No". He braced himself for rejection.

"I'd be happy to go with you, Zach."

"You would? Great! I can't believe it. You're so pretty, Marty." He truly meant that. In his eyes, Marty was the most beautiful girl in school. He loved to watch the way her red hair bounced when she walked and the brightness of her smile.

"Thank you, Zach."

She wanted to tell him that she thought he was 'hot,' as well, but felt it would be inappropriate, at this time, to do so. Instead, they became lost in a conversation that pertained to what they had planned to do after graduation: what colleges they each wanted to attend and what their career choices were.

Zachary told her that he was already committed to going to MIT to pursue engineering and design. His goal had been to design bridges, which he was fascinated with. He told her, enthusiastically, in detail, how they were built; the various steel enforcements and cables and how engineers experimented with chemicals and cement to get the maximum strength in order to withstand the weight of the many tons of vehicles.

Marty listened to his every word, intently. Most young women her age would have been bored to tears with the talk about formulas and foot pounds, but not her. She didn't care what he talked about, as long as he was talking to her. After telling her how embarrassed he was for going off on a tangent, Zach became silent. Marty told him not to worry; that she had been fascinated by his knowledge base.

To make her point, she told him what her plans were. She stated that she had wanted to attend Nazareth to become a nurse practitioner. She thought about becoming a doctor, but said that she was attracted to the nursing aspect of health care, because it was more of a 'hands on' career choice. Her love of medicine and helping the sick fascinated Zachary. He admired her extensive vocabulary and could practically see the intelligence pouring off of her.

They continued talking, passionately, about their career choices and then moved on to different topics: the drama of high school, music, and sports. Their likes and dislikes. They were both amazed at how similar their tastes were. Zachary was, inwardly, kicking himself for not having the courage to talk to her before this. He already liked the person she had become. They talked for nearly two hours, until Marty's father told her at ten o'clock she had to hang up the phone.

. . .

The night of the prom was more than Marty ever imagined it would be. In preparation for the big dance, she and

Stephanie spent a better part of the day doing each other's hair and make-up. Marty's mother had also done her part, spending hours, as well as a small fortune, shopping for the right dress.

The gown was a beautiful, full length, baby blue chiffon, with white lace around the cuffs and neckline. Matching high heels completed the ensemble. It had been Marty's first dance and Julia wanted to make it a special day for her daughter. Marty cried when they picked it out and hugged her mother, tightly. For Julia, that one gesture summed up parenthood and she would never forget the 'gift' her daughter gave to her. It was a mother/daughter moment she would cherish the rest of her life.

Zachary came to the door around 5:30 that evening to pick up his date. He was wearing a black, three-piece suit, complete with pinstripes. He looked like someone out of the "Godfather" movies, except he wasn't packing a weapon; at least Bill was pretty sure that he wasn't. After eyeing him up and down, he determined that the young man, taking his 'little girl' on her first date, was acceptable, although he never said so. Zach suffered through the numerous photographs her mother had taken, but he didn't complain. It was worth it to him. Marty was absolutely stunning.

As they were getting ready to leave, Julia, with tears in her eyes, hugged her daughter and wished the both of them a great evening. She looked at Bill and waited for him to say something nice, wiping her eyes. When it became obvious that he wouldn't, Julia gave him a gentle nudge with her elbow. She hoped that

Zachary hadn't seen it. If so, he never let on that he did.

Bill looked up into the eyes of the young man, shaking his hand and said, "It was a pleasure meeting you, Zachary. Take care of my little girl." Zach took Bills' hand, firmly into his massive one, letting him know that she was, indeed, in good hands. "It was a pleasure meeting you, too, sir." Then, waving a hand at Julia, he added, "Have a nice night, Mrs. Leonard."

"At least the kid has manners," Bill said, under his breath.

Julia folded her arms across her chest and raising an eyebrow, shook her head.

Bill raised his hands as if to say no harm no foul.

"What? What did I do?"

Zachary took Marty to a wonderful dinner at the Crimson Rose Café, in Penfield. Because neither one of them had been on a date before, Zach had thought it a good idea to go with another couple. Of course, Marty, naturally, had wanted to be with her friend, Stephanie. They were practically joined at the hip. Young Mr. Sharrow recognized that and had no objections.

Stephanie's date had been Brandon McPearson. The two of them had been 'going out' since the end of school the previous year, which was a record for Stephanie, at the time. Brandon was six-one and slender, having shoulder length, curly brown hair with

110

a hint of matching mustache. Outgoing and athletic, he played nearly every sport that Marion had to offer. Being that he was pretty good at most of them, Brandon had a tendency to be arrogant. He wasn't big, but he was very fast.

Brandon didn't know how to handle the quiet, reserved types, having nothing in common with them and finding them boring. When the girls excused themselves; not so much to check their make-up as to talk about the guys, Brandon hadn't said a word to Zachary. That was all right with him. He didn't have a great deal to say, anyway.

Once they had arrived to the prom, held in the cafeteria of the high school, Marty turned a great deal of heads, as usual. A few young ladies laughed when she walked into the room, but that had been short lived. They were no longer laughing once they saw their boyfriends staring at Marty. More than a few young gentlemen received a smack on the arm from a neglected young lady that night. All of them thought that Marty was beautiful and were in silent agreement—Zach Sharrow was a lucky man.

Marty wasn't voted the prom queen that night. In fact, her name had only been written on two ballots. Zach and Stephanie had both placed her name in the box decorated with pink and blue ribbon and bows. None of the girls wanted to vote for her and none of their dates dared. That had been fine with Marty. She was among friends and that was all that mattered to her. They danced, sang the lyrics to songs that they knew, and more importantly, had a great time together. Even Brandon was getting into it and started talking with Zachary more.

The title for queen went to Brianne Raes, which, in Marty's opinion, was a good choice. She was outgoing and seemed to get along with all of her classmates; that is except her. But, Marty hadn't been the slightest upset. She was having too good a time with her friends to worry about trivial matters and, eagerly went up to congratulate Brianne on her accomplishment.

It was no great surprise to Marty that, after the dance, a group of kids decided to go up to Chimney Bluffs near Sodus Point to 'hang out'. Most of them didn't have to be home until late and this included Zachary and Marty. At first, Bill had wanted his daughter home by midnight, but Julia told him to "Let her have some fun, for once." Bill reluctantly agreed.

Zachary was trustworthy. Even his father, beaming with pride, had let his son take the new Audi on his date. Tossing his son the keys with a wink, John Sharrow said, "Have a great time. Just don't scratch the paint."

Zachary asked Marty if she wanted to go to the bluffs and she eagerly said that she would like to. It wasn't love at first sight, but Marty liked Zach and knew there was something about him; something different, something wonderful. She trusted him, implicitly, and felt safe with him. He didn't disappoint her. Zach was a gentleman throughout the entire evening, opening the doors for her and placing his coat around her when she became chilled. She never had to worry that he would try anything.

112

The hazy, pre-dawn morning light was filtering through the clouds on the eastern horizon, after a clear, star-lit night, when the little party of 16 kids was becoming drowsy and decided to call it a night. Zachary extinguished the small fire he had started just after midnight, making sure that all of the coals had been put out by pouring water on them. He walked Marty to the car, opened the door, and waited for her to get completely settled before shutting it again. Climbing in the drivers' side, Zachary started the Audi and waited, patiently, for the others to whip out of the dirt parking area before heading out. He didn't want any rocks or gravel to be kicked up onto his fathers' car.

"Have a good time, Marty?" he yawned.

Zach watched her the whole evening. He had not been able to take his eyes off of her. He loved the way the warm glow of the firelight danced upon her flawless, milky complexion. Marty may not have felt the same way about Zachary, but he already knew that he loved her. For the first time in his life, he felt that he found someone that he could talk to; someone he was compatible with and liked the same things that he did.

"Yes, I did, Zach. It was one of the best days of my life. Thanks for everything."

"I had a great time, too," he replied as he put the Audi in drive and headed toward the main road.

"I didn't want this night to end. It was a beautiful evening: a little cold, but so calm and peaceful. It didn't take you long to build that fire, though."

"I guess being an eagle scout has paid off for something."

"I didn't know you were an eagle scout."

"It's something I don't tell everyone. It isn't popular being in the Boy Scouts, anymore."

"I think it's kinda cool. No one else had a fire."

Zachary turned onto the main road. Neither one of them spoke a word on the way home. Both were too tired to speak. Zach never took his eyes off of the road, the monotonous, yellow center lines wearing on him. Marty, even though she had started to doze off, was playing back memorable moments of the previous evening In her mind, like using the rewind button on the new VCR her parents bought. She had never been so content.

As Zachary pulled into her driveway, the rays of a full sun were beginning to shine through the newly budding birch trees, lining the property, on this early May morning. Spring had arrived. High school was nearly finished.

Marty awoke as soon as Zach turned the engine off. He actually wanted to watch her sleep for a while. In his eyes, she was so beautiful. But, as saddened as he had been that the date was over, he sprung out of the vehicle and opened the door for Marty.

"Well, we're home," he said, disappointed.

"Yah, we're home," she said, equally disappointed.

Zachary started to say something, but hesitated.

"Is there something you want to say, Zach?"

"I had a great time, tonight." He looked up at the sky "Last night," he corrected. "And I just wanted to know if I can call you, sometime?"

"I'd like that." Her smile was flawless.

Zachary could feel himself practically melting. He could never get tired of seeing that smile. He walked her to the front door. Marty gave him a small peck on the cheek and told him, again what a great time she had had. He took her petite hand into his and said that he hoped there would be more like it. Marty concurred. She quietly opened the door and stepped through.

Chapter VII

Marty's Choice

Because of Zachary's part time job at Bachman's market in Palmyra, as well as the demands of school, Marty hadn't been able to see much of him in the weeks following the prom. Although they had talked quite often by phone, they were only able to see each other twice, by the end of the month. What made matters worse Marty had also obtained employment, at Emerson's Drive-In, on 104, in Williamson. She wanted to save up some money, by the time she started college in the fall, to pay for books and other necessities she might need. She didn't particularly like waiting tables, but it kept her busy and gave her a little spending money. At least she wasn't sitting at home thinking about Zach.

Upon hearing that Marty Leonard had been seeing Zach Sharrow and working at Emerson's, Roger Van Dorn decided to pay a visit to the girl every guy had considered 'untouchable.' He figured that if that dweeb, Sharrow, could get Marty to go with him to the prom, it should be easy for him to get a date with her. Roger had seen Marty, in school, before he graduated the previous year. Like every other guy he knew, he considered himself unworthy and, being the coward that he was, never asked her out. But not that day. He washed his new Camaro, put on his leather vest, dabbed on some cologne, and headed toward

Williamson, to test the waters.

Marty saw the candy apple red Camaro pull into a parking spot close to the entrance door, but because she was attending to duties, did not see the driver get out of the vehicle. Roger walked through the door and immediately scanned the place, looking for her. She was facing the grill, filling napkin holders and did not see him come in, but, he, on the other hand, pegged her. "Can't miss that red hair," he mumbled to himself, as he walked over and sat down, strategically on a stool directly behind her.

Marty turned around to face the customer she had heard sit down behind her, pen and order booklet at the ready. She flipped the sheets to the next blank page and, looking up, said, "May I take your- hay, I know you. You're Roger Van Dorn, right?"

Pretending not to have noticed her when he came in, Roger said, "Yah. I think I know you from somewhere, too." Snapping his fingers for effect, as if it had just dawned on him where he knew her from, added, "Marty Leonard, from school. I haven't seen you in a long time. How have you been?"

"Good. Bet you're glad you're out of high school. How have you been?"

"Can't complain. Wouldn't matter if I did, anyway." Roger was full of old clichés.

118

An old Dodge pick-up pulled in next to Rogers' ride and two large men climbed down from the cab. Watching them from inside, Roger stated, "Don't scratch my paint, you clown."

"That's your car, Roger?"

"Yep. She's all mine. Just bought her three weeks ago," he said, beaming with pride. Actually, it had been Rogers' father who paid for most of it. "Would you like to come out and see her?" He added. The bait had been set.

"I'd love to, Roger, but I can't right now. I'm working," she said, stating the obvious.

"When do you get off work?" The line was in the water.

Marty glanced at the clock above the cash register. Disappointed, she replied, "Not for another forty minutes. Nine o'clock."

"Well, I was going to get something to eat, anyway. By the time I finish, you'll be ready to leave and then I could take you for a ride." The fish was looking. Girls always wanted to go for rides in a hot car.

"Really? I would love to go for a ride."

The manager, Scott Norton, gave Marty a signal for her to

hurry up, waving his hand in a circular motion and tapping his watch. He wasn't angry with her. It was part of the territory when you had a bunch of young teenagers working for you. It seemed like he was always having to keep employees motivated and on task.

"Well, it's settled. I'll wait for you to get off work and then we'll go for a ride." Fish hooked and ready to reel in.

"Great! Thanks," she said, not being able to hide her enthusiasm.

"Awesome. In the mean time, I'll have a double cheese burg, extra mayo and an order of onion rings. Oh, and I'll, also, have a large Coke with that."

Marty, still excited about her upcoming ride in Rogers' car, had not written his order. It wasn't that she was particularly interested in Roger, just his car. She had never been in a fast sports car before. Coming out of her daydream, Marty blurted, "I'm sorry. What was that you ordered?"

Roger repeated the order, smiling at her innocence. She smiled back at him and briskly walked toward the grill. He knew from this first conversation that Marty was a good girl; a girl that he would be proud to have in his life. He was determined, by any means necessary to make her his girl.

Roger took his time eating and still finished nearly 20

minutes before Marty finished her shift. He paid his bill, got into the Camaro and waited, not so patiently, for her to come out. It was something that Roger hated more than anything: waiting for something, or someone. He was not a patient young man. Everything had to go his way. But, on this occasion, Roger made an exception. He was willing to tolerate the inconvenience because he had an agenda and was after something of great value to him.

The sun had recently set as Marty came through the door just before nine. She took the clip out of her hair, letting it fall around her shoulders. She looked beautiful, to him. Roger started the engine and pushed the accelerator to the floor. The engine roared to life. Marty slid into the passenger seat and put on her seatbelt. Roger never bothered to open the door for her.

"This is a nice car, Roger," she said, rubbing the seat and dashboard. It was as if she was auditioning to be one of Barkers' Beauties modeling it on 'The Price Is Right.'

"Yah. She's my baby. Ready to go for a ride?" he asked, putting it in reverse.

"You bet I am. But don't go too fast."

"I won't," he lied.

Roger pulled out onto the main road; Route 104, heading east.

He was heading in the opposite direction from home, but it was less populated, meaning less traffic. Pushing it up to 80, he shifted smoothly and deliberately. Marty could hear the whine of the big engine and she started to get nervous. Yet, she couldn't help but feel the exhilaration from going at this rate of speed. She had never traveled this fast in her young life and it was evident; she had the need for speed.

Coming up, rapidly, behind a Cadillac Eldorado, Roger looked to see if anyone was coming the other way on the two-lane road and gunned the Chevy, easily maneuvering around it. He, just as effortlessly, swerved back into his lane and lowered his speed back down to 80.

"Wow. It handles great, Roger." Her voice elevated with excitement.

"She," he emphasized. "She handles great."

"What's HER name?" Marty asked, sarcastically.

"Roxanne. From that tune by the Police; she's fast and she is red," he stated, giving his stick shift a few pats.

"Oh. I'm not much of a fan of the Police." Then, realizing the time, said, "I'm having a great time, Roger, but I have to be getting home soon or my parents will worry."

"Ok, I'll turn around up here and head back." He tried to

sound disappointed. Roger was hoping he could get her to change her mind.

"I'm sorry, Roger, but if I am not home by 10 o'clock, my parents will think something happened."

He slowed the Camaro down and pulled into a driveway. Checking first for oncoming traffic, he backed out onto the road, heading in the direction he just came from and turned on his headlights. It was starting to get dark. Roger slowed the car on the return trip. He passed the same Cadillac that he had whipped by earlier, only this time, going an obedient fifty-five. Shortly after that, he passed a Wayne County sheriff going the opposite way. The sheriff gave Roger a quick glance and kept going, being that Roger wasn't breaking any laws, at the time.

"Glad he didn't see me about three minutes ago," Roger stated.

"You're not kidding." She too was relieved that they had not been pulled over. It would have made her late getting home. "They would have taken your license. You were going 80."

"Almost 90, when I passed that Caddy back there." Roger was afraid of losing his fish. They were only a couple minutes away from the restaurant. He had to act, quickly. "So, how do you like the ride?"

"Awesome. You have a great car, Roger."

"Would you like to ride in her again, sometime?"

"I'm seeing someone, right now, and I don't think it would be a good idea," she said, holding her head down and fidgeting with the hair clip she had placed in her lap.

Roger, noticing that Marty was uncomfortable with the conversation and where it was leading, took full advantage and asked, "Who's the lucky guy?"

"Zach Sharrow, although we don't get to see much of each other, between the demands of school and work."

"I can understand that," Roger told her. "It's difficult trying to make a go of a relationship when you can't see each other. It NEVER works out," he said, emphasizing the word 'never'.

"Well, I hope that isn't going to happen to us. Zach is so nice to me."

"I hope not, either," he lied. "Just be careful. A lot of things can happen when you are not around." It was nearly dark as he pulled back into Emerson's. There was only a thin halo of light visible on the western horizon. "Well, here we are."

Marty didn't say a word. What could she say? Roger only stated something that had been on her mind since she and Zach started seeing each other.

124

Roger pulled into the same parking space he had before they left. He could tell by the expression on her face that the statement he made was beginning to have their intended effect.

"Thanks, Roger," she said, sadly. Marty was, in fact, thinking about the statements he had made to her. She opened the door and got out, giving him a quick wave as she ran toward her parents' car.

"My pleasure, sweet cakes," he said, under his breath.

Roger was sure of one thing; that he had, at least scored a minor victory. He was positive that Marty was starting to question how much that idiot Sharrow really cared about her. That was all he could possibly had hoped for with the little time allowed. Moreover, he had placed his foot firmly in the door. Marty accepted the ride and talked to him. In Rogers' eyes, that meant that she liked him. He could accept this, for now. In order to cultivate the little interest she had in him, he decided to keep making himself visible to her by showing up at her place of employment every week to talk to the young woman he found to be absolutely gorgeous. Once Roger set his eyes on something, he was determined to get it.

The damage had, indeed, been done. Marty went home that night and began to think about how much time she and Zachary had actually been able to spend together since the prom. It wound up being less time than she had wanted to believe; a lot less: only a couple of hours per week. Her thoughts turned to college plans. Zachary was committed to MIT and she, on the other hand, had planned on attending Nazareth to be closer to home, although she hadn't finalized her decision. How did she expect a relationship to last a distance of over 500 miles? That was a six-hour drive, or more. She needed some input and, possibly, some advice on the matter. Marty thought she would run it by her mother and Stephanie.

Stephanie, always eager to talk about boys, told her that relationships could work over long distances depending on the individuals and how they felt about each other. Her mother, being more sensible, however, told her that it would be extremely difficult for two reasons. First: feelings can change the longer the two are apart. Her mother had called it the out-of- sight/out-of-mind factor. Since Marty and Zachary hadn't been seeing each other for very long, Julia said that it was highly unlikely that lasting feelings had developed. Second: college is a different world with many outside influences. The pressures of studies and peers are greater than high school and, either one or both could, very well, lose interest and find someone else. Julia told her that any number of things could happen. The odds were against them.

In the weeks ahead, Marty gave the subject a great deal of thought. As much as she wanted to believe what Stephanie had told her, she could see that her mothers' logic and insight had merit. Marty could see the truth in her mothers' words. It wasn't the fact that Zachary had treated her poorly. In fact, she never dreamed that she would be treated as well as Zach treated her. He

126

would do just about anything for her. It was just that Marty was afraid to put her all into the young relationship, only to be hurt in the end. "Wouldn't it be better," she thought, "to end the relationship, now, before feelings grew, than to work to build it only to get hurt, later?" This was the question that had plagued her thoughts for half the summer.

The week before graduation, Roger, as usual, had stopped by her work. It was a warm night and the first of the June bugs were coming out of the ground to feast on the different variety of leaves. Marty was still contemplating what, if anything, she should do about her relationship with Zachary when Roger walked through the door. Maybe, she thought, he might have some insight on what I should do. He had been right about the difficulties of having a relationship where the two involved never got to see each other; maybe, he would have further insight on cultivating a long distance relationship, as well. After mulling it over, Marty decided to run her predicament by him.

"I think your mother is right, Marty. Long distance relationships NEVER work out," Roger told her, again emphasizing the word 'never'. "Do you love him?" His curiosity was getting the better of him, but he wanted; needed to know her feelings. If she didn't love him, he knew that he had a good chance. He was hoping to better those odds.

"I don't know," she said, truthfully. "I, honestly, don't get the chance to see him that often to be able to tell you if I do, or not."

Roger respected her open candidness and liked the fact she was so naive. He found that the more he talked with her, the more he wanted to be with her. Believing he could be falling in love with the girl, Roger pressed on, digging for more information and thinking only of his own selfish gains.

"Well you're honest. That's good. You need to be honest with yourself, first. If you aren't sure if you love him or not, then you probably don't. You're young and pretty and extremely busy. Maybe, you need to concentrate on your studies or begin to see other guys."

"Zach is the first guy that has ever asked me out."

"I can't believe that," he said, trying to get a reaction. "I would give anything, including my car, to go out with someone like you."

"You would? But you could go out with any girl you wanted." Her lack of self-esteem was showing like the sun on that hot pre-summer day.

"Maybe, but I would like to go out with you. You have brains and you're pretty."

"I have to think about this, Roger. I don't want to hurt Zach, but I also don't want to be the one hurt, either."

"Fair enough. No pressure." He couldn't believe that he

was having this conversation with Marty. He knew he was getting close, but he, also, knew enough not to push it too far. That would be a sure way to lose the ground he had fought so hard to gain and he didn't want to blow it.

"I'll talk to Zachary more after graduation. If he still plans on going to MIT and doesn't really have a defined plan for us, I may just tell him that we shouldn't see each other and end it before one of us gets hurt. It may just be better to end it now, before we get too involved."

Roger couldn't believe what he was hearing. She had stated her fears in a calm, straightforward manner. He liked the fact that she was analytical and had everything so methodically thought out. "Maybe it is best, but either way, I'm going to give you the space you need." That was the second lie he told her. He had no intention of letting her have any space. He wanted her and he meant to have her.

.   .   .

Several weeks after graduation, Marty realized that she was the one that was going to have to perform 'the hurting'. She was sad, because Zachary was so good to her and had bent over backwards for her. There wasn't anything that he wouldn't do for her. It's just that his going away had bothered her. Marty asked Zachary if there was any way he could change his mind about going to MIT. He told her that it was one of the best engineering schools in the country and a fantastic opportunity for him. He told her that he realized it would be hard for them for a couple of years, but that once he was finished, he would be guaranteed a good paying job and would be more than able to support her. He wanted to marry her, but he was practical. He wanted to provide stability, as well as love.

Marty sat him down and broke the news to him as gently as she could, telling Zach that long distance relationships (using Rogers' term) never worked out. Zachary was in shock. What had he done, or better yet, hadn't done, to make her come to this decision. He pleaded with her not to break up with him, to no avail. He went home that evening devastated. He placed the Blue Topaz ring he had intended to give her on his dresser and hibernated in his room for a couple of days. He didn't even come out to eat.

No woman was ever going to come close to what he saw and felt in Marty. Other girls may want to date him in the future, but there wasn't a woman on the planet that was going to come close to her. She was beautiful, intelligent, loving, and compassionate...a total package. However, once the shock of being hurt was over with and he could give it some thought, he could honestly see how Marty had come to the conclusion.

Knowing just how intelligent she was, he realized that she must have analyzed the information many times over before finally coming to him. Her decision, even to him, seemed to be a

130

logical one. He was going to be away for between four and six years and that was an unreasonable amount of time to ask any girl to wait. Yet, that didn't help the fact that something was missing; something big, something irreplaceable. A void in his life materialized out of nowhere and he felt as if he had fallen into a great abyss.

Hoping that she changed her mind, he had called Marty several times over the summer. The answer had always been the same: sorry, but no.

Once he started school and especially after he had found out that she was seeing Roger Van Dorn, Zachary wanted to confront Marty, but that was not his style. He heard that she had put off going to Nazareth in order to stay closer to home and cultivate her relationship with him. Zach thought that she was making a huge mistake. But, he realized if he did that, he believed that he would only be making a fool of himself. Still, he wanted to tell her that Van Dorn was an arrogant, conceited control freak, who was, not nearly, good enough for her. That was the truth. Marty was just too good for the likes of Roger and he saw her relationship with him ending in complete disaster. Instead, he kept his distance. What would be the point? It had been made perfectly clear to him that she was not interested. Saying anything against Roger, at this time, would only make her believe that he was jealous and had an ulterior motive. As much as it hurt him to do so, he just let it go.

So, that left him with two huge questions. Where was he

going to find someone comparable? Where was he going to find someone compatible? Zachary Sharrow would spend the next 15 years searching for the woman who could answer those very questions.

Chapter VIII

Call to Rusty's

Marty was seated on the floor of the walk-in bedroom closet, tugging at one of Rogers' long sleeved, button down, flannel shirts, and cursing the fact that he had to have all of his shirts buttoned to the top when on a hanger. She didn't need the shirt because she felt cold. It was 96 degrees outside. Marty needed it because she had been in a state of undress, from the waist up, longer than at any time period in her life and wanted to have something on when the police and ambulance arrived. Marty felt that it would be easier, in her condition, to put on a flannel shirt. The flannel ones were all a size larger than his other shirts, because Roger had always worn them over other shirts during hunting season.

Looking down at her chest and abdomen, Marty could see that the dark purple bruises had become larger; telltale signs that there was some internal bleeding. "Is it only a soft-tissue bleed," she thought, "or are organs involved, as well?" She couldn't tell, and, in actuality, she didn't want to know. All she knew was that she had been in excruciating pain and didn't know how much more her body could take. Marty was just praying for enough time to accomplish what she had set out to.

For Marty, the last two hours of her life were the most painful she had ever experienced. The severity of pain she had, for as long as she had it, affected several body systems. Her mind had definitely been affected. It was so difficult for her to concentrate and stay focused. The simplest of thoughts needed to be checked and, sometimes, rechecked for accuracy. Her life depended on having good judgment. Her muscles began to tighten. The easiest of tasks caused them to lock up, quickly. She was, also, perspiring, profusely. But, the most embarrassing bodily function she had lost was bladder control. Marty felt wetness in her crotch and looked down to see a small, dark patch spreading on her faded blue jeans. She stared at it in disbelief. I can't believe I have just wet myself, she thought. A long grunt escaped her, out of anger. She wanted desperately to have this ordeal over and done with. How much longer could this go on? How much longer could she go on?

Marty resumed trying to get the shirt to come off the hanger, but it refused. She wasn't able to muster the force necessary to free it. The young woman grunted, again, as much out of frustration, this time, as pain. Why must everything be so damned difficult? Marty needed a shirt, but how was she going to get it? She had to find a stick. Where the hell am I going to get a stick inside a house, she thought? "Think, Marty," she scolded herself. Marty looked around the closet for something light enough for her to swing and knock down her prize. There had to be something in here she could use. She spotted it: something that would be able to serve two purposes. Leaning against the back wall, behind a stack of old magazines and a couple of board games, she saw exactly what she was looking for: the pair of crutches.

134

Maneuvering closer to those beautiful, aluminum supports, Marty hurriedly began pushing aside the magazines, to gain access to them. Once cleared, she stretched with all she had and reached for one of them with her right hand. Stretching caused pain. At this point, what didn't cause pain? Marty reached and was able to get a finger on the rubber handle. It began to move. It was almost in her grasp when it slowly started to list to one side and slide down the wall, crashing into a portable fan and ending up behind a rack of shoes. "NO! DAMN IT!" Couldn't one thing, at least, go right? No time to think about the loss. She had to make sure the same thing didn't happen to the second one.

Marty reached for the sister crutch, stretching her body as far as she could past the pile of magazines. Again, she could feel the rubber on her fingertips. It started to move. Not good. It stopped, momentarily, before slowly starting to move down the wall, like the first one. Marty was only going to get one shot at this. With everything she had, she lunged, bracing herself against the pain. She found the handle and tightly wrapped her fingers around it as if her life depended upon it. It may have. Carefully, Marty brought it closer to her body, never releasing the white-knuckled grip she had on it. Once it was close enough, she held it up, in triumph, as if it were a trophy.

Positioning herself in the center isle, far enough away from any obstacles, Marty took aim at the section of flannel shirts. Without thinking about it, she raised the crutch with all the strength she could muster and hit the jackpot. She could hear the tinkling of the metal hangers as two shirts fell to the floor. She could, also, hear a slight tear in her chest.

Once the pain subsided, she looked down and smiled at the two shirts. Marty was relieved. She saw stars. She knew, then, that if she did not get the shirt she needed on the first try, she was almost positive she would not have been able to raise the crutch, again. Finally, something had gone her way.

Marty wasted no time. She set the crutch on the floor next to her and went to work unbuttoning one of the shirts. A puzzling question came to mind. How am I going to get it on? It was followed by a second. Isn't this a great time to be asking myself that question? But, she couldn't raise her left arm above her head. In fact, it hurt to raise her elbow even a little. How was she going to put her arm through the sleeve and wrap it around her body to put her other arm in? I'm going to pass out, she thought. It seemed to her that for every dilemma she had been able to overcome, another problem popped up that needed solving.

"Leverage; I need leverage," she thought.

Marty needed a hard surface she could lean against to support her back. She scanned the closet and saw something that might work. Turning around, Marty backed up to the shoe rack, placing the shirt with the inside facing up on the floor next to her. She then placed her left hand in the opening of the sleeve and leaned her back against the rack. With her right hand, she was able to inch the garment up her left arm to her shoulder. She leaned forward and then back, again, pinning the shirt against the shoe rack. Reaching around the back of her neck with her right hand, she was able to grip the collar, bring it around, and slip her right arm through the other sleeve. Using only her good hand, Marty was able to pin the shirt against her chest and button it up. It was actually a piece of cake; much easier than she had thought possible and with minimal pain involved.

Marty had splinted her leg, made it downstairs without killing herself, and was able to dress. As a bonus, she had even talked to Stephanie. That meant that there was only one thing left on her mental agenda to do before Roger came home: load the rifle and get in a strategic position.

There it was. Standing at attention in the corner like a sentry, to the left of the entrance, eight feet away from her, was the Browning 30.06 A-bolt, semi-automatic rifle. She stared at it as if it were the Holy Grail. Time was getting short. Her heart began to beat faster as she scooted towards it, stopping only long enough to pick up the crutch she knew she was going to need, later. Then, she slid the rest of the way over to it and picking it up, as well, placed it, along with the crutch, effortlessly in her lap.

Leaving the closet with the new prizes she had obtained, Marty made her way over to Rogers' nightstand. The going was a bit cumbersome with the added weight and length of her tools. She opened the top drawer to the nightstand and fumbled for the magazine clip and box of ammo. From her position on the floor, Marty could not quite see into the drawer, but she knew approximately where to locate them. She pulled out a small box and looked at it. They were the long rifle bullets she had seen Roger, on many a hunting day, load into the weapon. Marty reached her hand back into the drawer feeling for the curved, flat, metal ammo clip. Success! She cupped it into her hand, squeezing it tightly, and brought it out.

Marty dumped the box of ammo onto the floor next to her. Then, loading three rounds into the clip, she slid it into the rifle, listening for the familiar click. It was in.

Making sure the safety was on Marty pulled back the bolt, allowing the first round to enter the chamber. With authority, Marty slammed it back into place. It felt good to do so. She felt another sharp twinge in her chest as the bolt finished its forward motion. Marty hardly noticed it. Her sense of purpose kept her focused. She was relieved and a little excited: she was officially armed and dangerous. More importantly, Marty was no longer vulnerable. An almost sinister smile came to her face. The odds had just been evened, considerably.

Marty made her way into the living room with a renewed sense of strength, although the strain from her injuries left her weak and tired. She was nearly spent. Because of the urgency, Marty hadn't given her injuries a moment's rest and they were letting her know it. She looked into the kitchen to see the time. The rooster clock above the sink read 4:12. Marty turned and

138

strained her neck to look out the front window. She could see enough to tell that Roger had not come home yet.

Marty now, had a different worry. She was physically exhausted and didn't know how long she could hold out. She had been on the verge of passing out, several times, and felt as if she was going to do so, again. She picked up the receiver out of its cradle and dialed, from memory, the number to Rusty's Roost. Marty was ready for the confrontation and she didn't know how long she would remain ready. She needed to end this as quickly as possible.

The room, suddenly, became dark. She thought she might be starting to black out, but realized that it was only the lack of sunlight as the massive cloud bank, coming in from the west, blocked its rays and blanketed the afternoon sky. Marty looked out of the window as Rusty picked up on the other end. She could see that the wind had started to pick up.

"Rusty's Roost. Rusty speaking," he said, testily.

"Hi, Rusty. This is Marty Van Dorn. Is Roger down there?"

Roger was just leaving. Rusty thought, briefly, to let him continue on out, but didn't feel right doing that to Marty. He knew that she was probably going to have to pay for his anger. Reluctantly, he said, "Yah, Marty, he's still here. I'll get him."

To Marty, it sounded like Rusty hadn't been happy at the mention of Rogers' name. There seemed to be a lot of that going around.

Marty could hear Rusty covering the phone and yelling for her husband in the background. Then, she heard it being placed onto something, a counter, perhaps. She waited for what seemed like an eternity for him to pick it up. Either he was playing pool and didn't want to be bothered, or he didn't think that she would call him and was ashamed to talk to her. She hoped it was the latter.

Roger was, indeed, in a state of shock. He froze, momentarily, not knowing whether to keep going or answer the call. Not only did he not believe she would call him there, he believed she wasn't going to be able to call anyone, ever again. The color drained from his face. What the hell was going on, he wondered? Could someone, that bitch Stephanie, maybe, have gone to the house and, finding the door unlocked, discovered Marty's body and decided to call him there to tell him it was over for him? How would she have known where to find him? No, there seemed to be only one logical explanation. Since it couldn't be Stephanie and the dead couldn't talk, it had to be Marty.

Roger walked towards the phone at a much slower pace than he did when leaving. He looked at it as if there might have been some kind of trap waiting for him. Rusty noticed the color drain from his face. He knew something was wrong.

Picking up the receiver, Roger held it to his ear, wondering how she was going to sound. Would it be a raspy, hoarse, laryngitis sort of thing, or more like a gurgling, drowning in liquid sound? Only one way to find out.

"H-Hello," he said, unable to prevent his voice from cracking.

"Hello, Roger." An angry sounding Marty Van Dorn greeted her husband. Except for the lisp, she sounded perfectly healthy. How could that be? He tried to act natural, as if nothing was amiss, but from the way Rusty was looking at him, he wasn't doing a good job. All he could think about, as she was speaking, was, "This isn't good. What the hell am I going to do, now?"

Hearing Rogers' voice cracking and knowing she was armed, Marty, believed she had finally achieved the upper hand. She confidently told him "Don't say a word. You WILL not enter this house. You WILL stay on the walkway. You WILL listen to everything I have to say or I am going to blow your head off. You got that? It's over, Roger." Click.

Roger had been nodding his head the whole time, although Marty wasn't able to see it. It was priceless. Had it not been for the circumstances, she would have found it rather amusing, since he was the type of man that didn't put up with anything even close to that coming from a woman, much less his own wife.

Still holding the phone to his ear listening to a dial tone, Roger tried to sound as if Marty was still on the other end of the line. He pretended that she had been giving him a list of things to pick up at the store, on the way home. He picked up a pen and jotted a word on the notepad lying next to the phone. He ripped the top sheet off, folded it, and placed it in his shirt pocket. Then, he set the pen back down on the counter.

The more he thought about what Marty had said and, more importantly, how she had presented it, the angrier he became. The question that came to mind was how to get home and finish the job. He knew, for certain, he had no choice.

Other than the fact that she had sounded pissed off and had a lisp, Marty sounded perfectly normal. She didn't sound, at all, like a woman in distress. Not good. He knew what he had to do, but he didn't know how he was going to be able to do it? "This may be more of a challenge," he thought. "Be home, soon," he said, lowering the receiver to hang up.

Intuitively, Rusty, who had been half-listening and not liking, at all, the smirk on Rogers' face, asked, "Is everything all right, Rog?"

Not even bothering to look at him, he started towards the door and replied, "Fine. Everything's fine."

Wanting to know what it was that Roger had written

down, Rusty went to the next sheet of paper. He could see the indentations of letters, as he held it up to the light, but still couldn't make out the word. He took a pencil and lightly went over the tiny depressions, back and forth, and then held the paper back up to the light. In capital letters, "RIFLE." He stared at it in disbelief. He lowered it, again, and glanced toward the door. "Oh, my God."

Chapter IX

Class Reunion

Marty placed the rifle in the recliner and leaned the crutch against the end table next to it. Then, she carefully lifted herself into the chair, as well. Debating whether or not to even risk further injury, Marty reasoned that the recliner would provide the best vantage point, as well as some much-needed comfort. She couldn't see everything she needed to from a seated position on the floor. Digging her lovely nails into the cloth fabric on the arm of the chair, she worked herself into a kneeling position on her good leg. Once there, she was able to really dig deep into the armrest and push with her left foot. She liked the recliner, but actually didn't care about damaging it. It was Rogers' favorite chair.

More pain. Marty could hear the fabric tear as she struggled to lift herself in. With a great deal of effort, she was able to turn her body, slowly around and sit down. The room was spinning. But, for the first time since before her merciless beating, Marty was in a comfortable place. She took a long deep sigh and closed her good eye, hoping that the room would soon stop turning. It was amazing to her how much easier everything was when you were healthy and uninjured. Nothing was convenient.

Yet, even though the nightmare was almost over, Marty

knew that she was, definitely, not out of the woods, yet. Her mental status was in a state of decline because of the pain she had been in and the length of time she had been in it. She, also, started to feel pain in her abdomen. That can't be good, she thought. She ran the events of the afternoon back through her mind and was amazed that she had made it so far. "I should have passed out, by now. I must have an extremely high tolerance for pain." There was still one more thing left to do. "Better get to it."

Using the end of the barrel of her Lil' friend, as Pacino called his weapon in 'Scarface', she was just able to lift the window enough to get the barrel of the 30:06 through. She rested the rifle barrel on the sill and placed the butt of it on the back of the recliner. Then, she wiggled around to get into a more comfortable position. She knew it was going to take Roger approximately fifteen minutes to get home, so she wanted to relax, collect her thoughts, and finalize her plan.

The chair was on a swivel. She turned it toward the end table, picked up the phone receiver glad that it was cordless and placed it in her lap. She looked at her weapon to make sure the safety was still on. It was. Marty never noticed it before, never really cared, but the rifle was, truly, a sharp looking weapon; polished silver barrel, beautiful wood-grained finish, and a sleek, jet-black scope to complete the package. A beauty. Too bad, she thought, that something so pretty had to be used for the purpose of taking a life; whether it was animal or human. She began to think about it in depth.

146

It wasn't that Marty thought the pain would be too unbearable for her to fire the rifle; she had already factored in the wicked recoil. Examining her own conscious, Marty hadn't fully thought about the consequences, until now. Unlike Roger a few hours earlier, Marty retained rational thinking and even picturing in her mind what would happen if she actually had to pull the trigger. She pictured him, lying on the walkway, in a pool of blood, pictured the police questioning her and taking her away. Marty sat back in the chair. "I can't do this," she whispered.

Marty realized that there was no way she was going to be able to pull the trigger if Roger had thought to come in after her. She couldn't have that on her conscious. Stephanie had been right. She had been angry and emotionally charged when she talked to her. Marty was going to have to trust that the police were going to get to her before he did.

What came to mind, next, startled her into action. Marty had forgotten to check the door to see if it was locked. Looking over at the doorknob, she could see that the latch was vertical. It wasn't locked. Damn. She had just made herself semi-comfortable. More pain. Would this ordeal ever end? Climbing down from her perch, she scooted toward the door with a sense of urgency. Reaching up with her right hand, she turned the latch to the horizontal, locked position.

In tears, out of both pain and frustration, Marty made her way back to the chair and started the process of getting back into it, all over again. At least the holes in the armrests were already there. After a few moments, she was back into the recliner, heart pounding and winded, with her leg out straight in front of her. She was very close to the breaking point.

.   .   .

"Hurry up, Roger," Marty said, exasperated with her husband.

"All right, all right. A man's gotta look good, too y'know. Remember I know most of your classmates as well as you do."

"Well, it always seems that we're late for the things I have to do."

"You're so imagining things. I'm usually ready for everything and you are the one primping and putting on your make-up."

"Oh, please, Roger. When we visited mom last year, you procrastinated getting ready until the last minute and we wound up being two hours late."

Roger rolled his eyes. "Your mother doesn't like me, that's why. But, I'm usually ready for everything else you need to do."

148

Marty knew that there was no use arguing with the man. In his mind he was always right. Since this was her 15-year class reunion, she simply let it go. They would be a half hour late, but arguing would only make him not want to go at all. It wasn't worth the aggravation.

They arrived at Brownstone Country Club, in Ontario at around 7:30. Roger, knowing that the bar was open only an hour before dinner, parked the truck and ran for the door. He didn't bother opening the door for Marty. It was hard for her to climb down from the truck cab in high heels, but she had grown accustomed to doing everything for herself. Marty wanted to take the wagon, but Roger, not wanting to look un-cool, insisted on taking the Silverado. It was all about the looks.

Roger walked up to the bar and sat down at the last remaining open barstool and ordered a Coors' for himself and a white wine for Marty. At least he didn't make her buy her own drink.

"Hey, Roger. I thought that was you. Where's Marty? It was Jack DeRoche. Roger hadn't seen him in over ten years. He had decided to join the Air Force after he had lost his inspector's position at Finger Lakes Foods, due to downsizing, in the fall of '95. Jack was obviously on leave because he had that high-and-tight military-style haircut.

"She's coming. She just wanted to hang up her shawl first. I told her I'd order a couple a drinks." It was astounding how easy it was for Roger to lie without batting an eye.

The bartender placed two coasters in front of Roger and set a glass of wine on one of them and a tall, empty beer glass on the other. He then poured the Coors' into the glass, leaving a half-inch head on it. "That'll be six-fifty," he said.

Roger took a $10 bill out of his wallet and handed it to him.

"Be right back with the change"

"I haven't seen you in ages, Rog. How've you been?" Jack asked him.

Picking up his beer, he said, "I'll be better when I get a couple a these in me. How 'bout yourself?" He didn't particularly care how Jack was. Just another lie. The beer was more important to Roger.

"I'm good. I'm stationed at Ramstein Air Base, Germany, now. I'm a tech sergeant. Made rank rather quickly," Jack stated. He was proud of his accomplishment.

"Great."

"You still got that '91 Camaro? That was a machine."

"No. Sold it a couple a years ago. I needed something a

little more practical, so I bought a Chevy Silverado."

"Nice."

The bartender came back and set $3.50 in change on the bar and started to walk away. Roger took several big gulps of beer and ordered another one.

"That was sure some good lookin' automobile you had there, Roger."

"Thanks. She sure was."

The truth was, Roger really did miss that car. He had spent more time with that Camaro than he did with Marty or anyone else, combined.

"We sure had some good times, back then."

Marty walked into the room and the eyes were upon her, instantly. After 15 years, she was still a stunning woman. She spotted Roger at the bar and started towards him, shawl still wrapped around her shoulders. Roger noticed it at once and had to think, quickly, to cover up his lie.

"You didn't hang up your shawl, hon?"

"I thought it might be a little chilly in here. You know how these places like to turn up the air, sometimes. Oh well."

151

"You can always put it on the back of a chair or hang it up later." Then he added, "You remember Jack DeRoche, don't you?"

"Jack. Hi. I didn't recognize you without all that hair you used to have. How's military life?"

"Good. I can't speak for everyone, but the Air Force has been great to me."

Jack was one of the guys who had come around after high school was over. He had been the class clown and got along with everyone. Everybody liked Jack. He was a character: quick with a joke and easy going. Since Roger didn't offer his stool to his wife, Jack got up and offered his, making an excuse that he had to visit other old friends. He was surprised that Roger hadn't gotten up to allow Marty to have his place. He set his half-empty beer on the counter and walked toward the restroom, fairly annoyed.

"It's nice seeing Jack after all these years, isn't it Roger?"

"If you say so," he said, taking another long swallow.

Just then, Stephanie came running up to her, giving her a huge, sisterly hug. "Marty, how are you? I didn't see you come in. I'm glad you made it."

"Wouldn't have missed this for the world," Marty stated. "I can't believe it's been 15 years, already."

"I know. Where did the time go?"

Roger turned to nurse his second beer, not caring too much for the girl talk. Besides, he never really cared for Stephanie anyway. He knew that she always filled Marty's head with garbage and that had been the reason why he discouraged her from visiting very often. Stephanie never acknowledged Roger's presence, which pissed him off, royally. For her, the feeling was, more than, mutual.

Stephanie was followed by her husband, Drake. He was nothing like the man Marty had pictured her marrying, but she liked him. He was tall and lanky- kind of a nerdy character. However, he was extremely intelligent and good-natured. Drake wore glasses with thick round lenses on his long, pointed nose to correct his near-sighted vision. Overall, Marty thought he was a good choice for Stephanie. She wasn't as hyper as she was in school and he always treated her like a precious gem. They had always done everything together and rarely had an argument. More importantly, Drake never laid a hand on her.

"You remember my husband Drake."

"Absolutely. Hi Drake, how are you?" she stated, shaking his hand.

"I'm Great. Beautiful evening. Beautiful wife. What could be better?" He gave Stephanie a hug and glanced toward Roger.

Roger half turned and did not acknowledge the comment. He was already bored with the man.

"Roger, this is Stephanie's husband, Drake."

"Swell." Roger didn't even hold out a hand to shake Drake's open one.

Drake put his hand down and stated, "Well, would you like to join us at our table? Dinner should be starting shortly."

Marty tried to make light of the situation and eagerly accepted Drake's invitation before Roger could say "No." She latched onto Stephanie's arm as they walked to their table.

Roger stayed to finish his beer and ordered one to take with him. "This is going to be a fun evening."

Chapter X

Dinner at Eight

The Van Dorns sat down with the Staffords to a wonderfully prepared Prime Rib dinner. It was cooked to perfection. Roger was able to get the end cut he wanted, as usual. He always seemed to get everything he wanted, no matter what it was. Marty, because she was continually watching her intake, asked for a thinner cut, but, it too, was done the way she liked it; medium rare.

Roger ate his dinner rather quickly and made a fast getaway to the bar, so as not to be bored to death with the niceties of conversation. He had more in common with the beer he would soon be consuming. Whatever Drake—and Roger couldn't help but associate his name with ducks—talked about was way over his head and didn't interest him, in the least. He couldn't even pretend to like the guy. For Roger, nothing worse than to be bored stiff by a duck.

Roger didn't even excuse himself, just, rudely, gave a slight nod as he turned and walked briskly to the bar. Of course, Stephanie couldn't help but make a snide comment, under her breath, as Roger was leaving. Marty didn't quite catch the remark she made about her husband, but knew it was derogatory, in nature. What ever it was, Marty knew that Stephanie had been right and she was highly disappointed with Rogers' actions.

An awkward silence lingered with the remaining party of three. Stephanie was just about ready to break it by asking Marty if she thought Zachary Sharrow was going to show when she looked up and saw him leaning on the entrance doorway. She gave Marty a nudge with her elbow and pointed at him. Marty looked up and seeing Stephanie pointing turned to look in that direction. Marty shook her head. After all these years Zachary had not changed a bit. He was still shy and looked slightly out of place. He was dressed casually, enough, and looked good in his sport jacket and tie, but as she remembered, he seemed uncomfortable in his surroundings.

Stephanie, always observant, stated, "He hasn't brought anyone."

Marty didn't say anything and, looking down at her utensils, started cutting another slice of meat.

Stephanie leaned over and whispered something to her husband. He nodded in the affirmative and, just like that, she was gone like a shot.

Drake was not the jealous type and understood that Stephanie was bound to meet up with old friends and old boyfriends, even. That was the reason for having class reunions. Besides, she had been more than tolerant of his old friends when the two of them went to his class reunion several years back.

As Stephanie was getting up to leave, Marty, knowing that she was up to something, put a hand out, in a feeble attempt to stop her. It was much too late. All she could do was watch as Stephanie half-sprinted across the room toward Zach. She turned to Drake, gave him an awkward smile and pretended to eat her dinner. In no way was she going to be able to finish it. She was too nervous.

As usual, Zachary showed up late for the festivities. Zach was late for nearly every social activity, at this stage in his life, but, this time, he wasn't sure he wanted to show up at all. After 15 years, he knew it was still going to be painful for him to look at Marty. The summer after high school was still fresh in his mind, as if it had just happened the day before. He still had feelings for her. Not only that, he hadn't kept in touch with any of his old classmates. He never even kept in contact with the guys on the basketball team. They had gone to sectionals the year they graduated and had made it to the Section V title game for the first time in nearly 20 years. They missed taking it all by four points.

Zachary was leaning against the doorway: the loner scanning the room, contemplating whether or not to leave. He had nothing in common with these people, anymore, and felt totally out of place. He was about ready to turn and head out the same door he had just entered, moments prior, when he saw Stephanie half-running and weaving around others, trying to get to him. It was very amusing to see her trying to sprint across the length of the floor in high heels. He was thinking the Olympic committee should make an event out of that: the 100-yard high-heel dash.

"Zach Sharrow, you finally made it," Stephanie screamed, wrapping her arms around him and nearly knocking them both to the floor.

Once he regained his footing and had helped her do the same, Zach said, "Well, well. Stephanie Dawson. Nice to see you. To be honest with you, I hadn't planned on coming."

"It's Stafford, now. I got married."

"Oh, I'm sorry. I mean I'm sorry I didn't know, not I'm sorry that you are married."

"It's okay, Zach. I knew what you meant. So, tell me, what are you doing, these days? I haven't seen you in so long."

"Oh, I keep pretty busy. I'm an engineer, working for the state designing and supervising the building of bridges. It was something I had always wanted to do and I am fortunate to be in the position I am. We just completed the Millennium Bridge in Rochester."

"You did that?"

"Well, I helped design it. It takes a whole team to build it."

"That's wonderful, Zach. I always knew you were going to succeed and do something great, in life."

"Well, I don't know how great it is, but I sure love what I am doing." Then, his curiosity getting the better of him, he added, "By the way, is she here, Marty, I mean?"

He almost feared the answer. He had a need to see her, yet at the same time, he knew that she was still married and didn't want to put himself through the emotional roller coaster. The pain from their break-up was as fresh in his mind as if it had happened a week prior. It was disturbing to him. He had been upset with himself for the last 15 years about not being able to let go. How could he possibly have feelings for a woman he hadn't seen in a decade and a half and dated only a couple of times? He spent as many years trying to make sense of it all.

"Yes, she is and, of course, Roger is with her." She sounded as disappointed as he was.

"I more than figured that and I won't bother her. Part of me wants to see her again." He sighed. "And part of me doesn't."

"I know, but I'm sure that she would like to see you though."

"I may stop and say hello, but it will probably be uncomfortable for her. I know it will be for me, come to think of it."

Trying to coax him, Stephanie said, "Come on over to our table for a moment. Roger left for the bar a few minutes, ago."

"I don't know," Zach said, looking down at his feet.

"Come on, just say hello to her."

"Maybe for a minute."

The two of them walked to a little table toward the back of the room to join Drake and Marty. Roger, by then, had stopped drinking beer and had moved up to Bacardi and Coke. He was still at the bar.

While Marty continued to fuss with her plate and pretend to be eating, Stephanie, formally, introduced Zachary to her husband. As much as he had wanted to get a glimpse of Marty, Zachary fought the urge and stuck out a massive hand to shake Drake's. He, not only wanted to be polite, he didn't want to seem too anxious to see Marty. "Glad to meet you, Drake."

"Pleasure," Drake said, in return.

Turning to face Marty, he said, "And you don't need to introduce this lady to me. How are you, Marty? It's been a long time." It was a lame cliché, but he couldn't think of anything else to say.

It had been an awkward moment for the both of them, but Marty managed a meek reply. "I'm good."

Zach held her petite hand between the two of his large ones and, unconsciously, began to gently rub it. He didn't want to stay and yet, he had felt compelled to do so. She didn't pull away. He could feel his stomach tighten. She was still beautiful, to him, just as he envisioned she would be. He always wondered what it would be like to see her, again, but never thought he would be given the opportunity. Now that he was face to face with her, he didn't know what to say. He wasn't even thinking; just kind of went with what was in his heart, when he said, "You look as lovely, as you always have. The last 15 years have been very good to you."

"Thank you, Zachary," she said, making eye contact with him for the first time. "You look great, yourself."

"You didn't bring anyone, Zach?" Stephanie inquired.

"No. I just haven't been able to find anyone who would put up with me," he said, never taking his eyes off Marty.

Seeing those eyes, those beautiful hazel eyes, made him want to melt into the woodwork and he realized that he could no longer do this to either one of them. She was stunning. It was a rather large banquet room, but he still felt as if the walls were beginning to close in on him. He needed to get away. "Well, I guess I had better be going. You all have a nice dinner. I'm going to get something to eat before they close the buffet. Take care of yourself, Marty. Nice meeting you, Drake. Bye, Stephanie." And reluctantly, with a final squeeze of her soft, beautiful hand, Zachary was gone.

As soon as he had been out of ear shot, Marty was finally able to manage, "You too, Zach."

Roger, upon seeing Zachary leaving the table, took the last half of his Rum and Coke in one gulp and slammed the glass down onto the bar. He swaggered over to his wife's side and said, "Was that dweeb boy, Sharrow?"

On the verge of tears, Marty picked up her napkin, wiped her mouth with it, and excused herself, saying that she had to use the ladies room. Stephanie, after giving Roger a look of contempt, got up and followed Marty.

Roger, so wanted to hit her, but knew better than to do something like that in such a fine dining establishment, with her husband sitting only a few feet away. But, there may come a day, woman, he thought, when you're going to cross me at the wrong place and time, when there aren't going to be any people around to save you. Then you're gonna pay, dearly.

It wasn't that Marty believed that she had feelings for Zachary. She, honestly, no longer knew him. She was practical. Too many years had passed since the last time she had seen him and she didn't know him well enough to begin with. Besides that,

162

she was married; end of discussion. What brought tears to her eyes was the realization that she had married the wrong man, but not that Zachary had been, necessarily, the right man. Roger was an embarrassment. He was uncouth at times, and slovenly most others. He was ill-tempered and she was tired and frustrated with not being able to make her own decisions or go out with friends and have a good time, without the fear of what Roger was going to say or do to ruin the occasion.

After trying to comfort Marty, to no avail, Stephanie had left her alone in the ladies room to search for Zachary. She was hoping that he hadn't left, yet. Knowing how much Zach had remained the same over the years; she thought it to be a serious possibility and quickened her pace.

She glanced over to her husband, who was, at that time, alone at the table and held up an index finger as if to say "Just one minute." Drake gave her the 'okay' sign, not caring one bit. He was attacking a nice big piece of chocolate cake.

Luckily, Stephanie's search didn't take long. She found Zachary sitting by himself, at a dimly lit table, in the far corner of the room. He was facing the wall, eating the remainder of his dinner. I have already paid for this, he thought, might as well eat. Mr. Sharrow planned on making a quick exit, as soon as he was finished.

He had heard her walking up to him before he saw her. "I knew it was a bad idea coming here, tonight. It wasn't worth the money I spent on the dinner. I should have stayed home with the dog."

"No, Zach, it wasn't a bad idea. Can I sit down for a minute?"

"I don't believe any of these seats are taken," he said, gesturing at the five empty chairs around the table. "I don't see why not. Nobody is going to complain."

Stephanie sat down in the nearest one to him. "Listen, Marty and I have always been close. We're not as close as we were in school, but we're still close. Roger is the reason why we're not. Marty has confided in me and told me that he has hit her, on several occasions."

Zachary looked shocked. He did not know how to respond to that.

"I know. It was a shock to me too. It is because of that reason I don't go over there very often. She isn't allowed to come over to my house very often and I can't stomach being in his presence, so I stay away. I just can't watch her suffer like that."

Zachary couldn't say anything. He just shook his head and pushed his plate toward the center of the table. He no longer had an appetite.

"I don't know what to do for her, Zach. She needs a

friend more than ever, but I have my own family to worry about. I can't bring my two little ones over there. What if that idiot goes ballistic? I have talked with her about calling the police on him. She has not been very receptive. And if I call them, she will never speak to me again. She wants somebody to listen to her, but she also wants to handle things herself."

The more Stephanie revealed, the angrier he became. Zachary was boiling, inside. He was always a gentleman and had never laid a hand on any woman. His father had always told him that hitting a woman was the most cowardly act a man could do. The longer he sat there, thinking about it, the more upset he became. He clenched his gigantic hands into tight fists and his face became flushed. He shook his head, wanting to do something but not knowing what.

Zachary scanned the room and spotted the, by now, unsteady Roger Van Dorn, talking with Dan Erickson. Erickson was an obnoxious kid in school that had the same interest in cars, back then, as that jerk did. Zach glared at them.

Stephanie knew she hit a nerve and sat back in her chair. She had a scared look on her face. She didn't know if Zachary was going to get up and deck him.

Looking back at Stephanie and seeing the fear in her eyes, he slowly unclenched his fists and ran a hand through his thick hair. "It isn't worth it, Stephanie. I'm not going to hit him; not here, at least. I never liked that bastard in school and I sure don't like him, now. I always thought that he was an arrogant piece of trash that wasn't worth my time. He still isn't worth it." He paused, reaching into his back pocket for his wallet. "Look, I have to get outta here before I lose control. Here is my card. It has my work number on it. I wrote my home number on the back. If you, or Marty need anything, don't hesitate to call me."

"I won't, Zachary. I have a feeling that I'll be calling you, soon."

"It was great seeing both you and Marty, again," he said, taking his jacket, which he had neatly draped over the back of his chair. "I mean it. Call me. I have friends down town who can possibly help Marty."

Stephanie couldn't help but feel that she had, somehow, betrayed Marty's trust. At this point in their lives, they were no longer best friends; they were 'life' friends. Even though they didn't get to see each other very often, they had a friendship that had stood the test of time. She didn't tell Zachary any of this in order to hurt Marty, but only because she had run out of answers and was afraid of losing her. She felt that something bad was going to happen, and very soon.

Stephanie always admired and respected Zach. There was something about him, something noble, chivalric, even. She smiled to herself. She saw Zachary as a true, gentlemanly knight, who would wind up coming to the damsels aid and save her in the nick of time. That damsel just happened to be her best friend.

166

Stephanie turned the card that Zach Sharrow had given her over to the front side. Along with the picture of a suspension bridge, were his office address and phone number. It was rather plain, but something she would have expected, coming from him: no frills and to the point. Then, she realized something. It was the second time in 15 years that Zachary had handed her his number.

Chapter XI

Roger Returns

The storm was gaining strength all around her. Lightning strikes were becoming closer and more frequent by the minute and an eerie, orange glow had appeared in the late sky, around the rolling cloudbank. Marty had never seen a storm this black and ominous looking, before. The wind intensified, quickly, as she watched the cold front plow through. It was nearly upon her. A small branch, from the last remaining birch tree in the yard, broke off and flew past the window, spinning wildly. Marty turned to look at the clock on the wall in the kitchen. It was 4:32. Roger, even in this weather, should be home, shortly.

The temperature outside had dropped thirteen degrees in less than a half hour, cooling things off dramatically. Marty could feel the wind through the two-inch crack in the window where she had placed the rifle. Drops of rain started to fall from the first clouds to come over the property. They were infrequent, but huge, hitting the patio deck with a noticeable hard smack. This was going to be a bad storm and she knew it.

Marty saw headlights coming down the road. As they came closer, she could tell that it was Roger's truck. "Looks like you're going to get soaked, Roger," she said, reaching for the phone in her lap. The truck started slowing down as she hit the power button on the phone. Suddenly, a bright flash of light filled the room. A loud boom, sounding more like an explosion, let her know that it had been a very close strike. The light on the barn across the street flickered once, sparked, and blew out, showering the road with glass. Everything that ran on electricity ceased functioning. The house became silent; no refrigerator motor, no AC in the bedroom, no clock, nothing. Dead silence. "Oh no, the phone."

Quickly, she brought the receiver up to her ear. No dial tone. Marty switched it off and turned it back on again. Still nothing. Panic set in. This isn't happening, she thought. After all that had transpired during the last several hours, everything she had to endure, now, this? A look of sheer terror came to her face as she realized the implications. She had lost her lifeline.

As Marty looked out of the front window, she noticed that the clouds were swirling in a pattern that she had never seen before. They were turning into themselves in a circular motion. Then, she saw something even more bizarre. She watched as Roger turned into the dock area of the barn. Marty continued to watch and witnessed Roger get out of the truck, walk purposefully up the steps, and disappear into the barn. "Why was he doing that?" she thought. Maybe he was going to wait out the storm in the barn. That will be good, she thought. The electricity may come back on, by then, and I can call the police. How ironic. A few minutes prior, Marty couldn't wait for Roger to come home so that she could get this over with. With the storm knocking out the power to the house and her ten-digit

170

savior, she was hoping for more time until it came back on.

.   .   .

Roger left the bar and was looking up at the late afternoon sky. "Looks like rain. We could use some." He walked, purposefully, back to his truck, opened the drivers' side door, and climbed in. Then, he fumbled in the glove compartment for a pack of smokes. He pulled out a pack of cigarettes and dug the lighter out of the cup holder. It was one of those cheap throw away kind, but it served the purpose. Marty didn't like him smoking in the house and it was one of the few things he had conceded to. He felt that she was right. He didn't like being in a smoke filled room, either. But, that was going to change. Other things were going to change, as well.

Leaning against the Silverado, Roger lit a cigarette and took a long, mind-soothing drag, holding it between his thumb and index finger. He was quietly resolved, knowing exactly what needed to be done, but not knowing precisely how to go about it. Roger had to finish the job he had thought he finished a few hours back. How? He took another drag from the cig, trying to clear his head.

Speaking of how, he thought, how the hell did she survive such a beating? I gave her everything I had and it sounds like I barely scratched her. How is that possible? I knocked teeth out. I heard bones break. I gave the bitch everything I had. What the hell is going on here? The longer he thought about it, the angrier he became. Roger shook his head and took another drag, not bothering to flick the ashes away.

"Wait-a-damn-minute!"

Roger remembered hearing something from upstairs before he left the house; remembered standing at the door, listening for any other sounds, believing he was only hearing things, before deciding to leave. At the time, it had actually creeped him out, a bit. "How could I have been so stupid?" he said, hitting his forehead. Why didn't I go up there and check it out."

A young couple strolled past Roger on their way into the bar, holding hands. Noticing how angry he was, they didn't bother saying anything to him. They thought he was intoxicated and figured it best not to agitate the angry drunk any further. Mind your own business and keep on walking. As they reached the door, the young man opened it for his girl, but could not resist temptation and took a glance in Roger's direction. Taking offence to that, Roger yelled, "What the hell are you lookin' at, boy?" The young man didn't acknowledge with a reply and wisely followed his date inside.

"Roger, telephone," he said, mocking the way Rusty had called him back to take Marty's phone call. Then, it hit him. "She didn't tell Rusty I beat the hell out of her. She must want to confront me. That's why she won't let me in the house. In all probability, that means she hasn't called the police, either. Well, if she wants a confrontation, I'll give it to her."

Roger took the last hit off the cigarette. He threw it to the ground, and stepped on it, twisting it under his boot. Looking up at the fast-approaching cloudbank, he opened the door to the cab and climbed back in. He wanted to race home, before the storm rolled in. Already, he could feel that the temperature had fallen, considerably. Not only that, he had some unfinished business to attend to. Roger started the engine and punched the accelerator, spitting up stone and gravel, as he left.

Once on the open road, Roger could see a panoramic view of just how massive the storm was. Turning east onto Shilling road, he was thinking that he had never seen clouds swirling like they were or a sky so orange. Flashes of lightning filled his rear-view mirror only a couple miles behind him. The storm was gaining fast. Roger stepped on the gas, hoping to outrun it.

Roger turned left and then a quick right onto the old Hydesville Road, tires squealing. His thoughts returned to how he was going to finish Marty off. Roger was no longer concerned with getting caught. He already believed that getting caught was a real possibility and since that was the case, felt that he no longer had to be careful. If he was going down, he intended to take her with him.

Neatness no longer mattered. He could finish the job any way he chose. It was added to a growing list of things that no

173

longer seemed to matter. He just wanted to take care of things once and for all. He hated to lose.

The rifle and shotgun were in the house and he knew that Marty had, at least, one of them loaded. She stated that she was going to blow his head off if he tried to come into the house. "I'll be DAMNED if I'm going to let her win," he hotly stated, pounding his fist on the dashboard.

The first rain drops, big, heavy ones started to pummel the windshield, as he turned onto Sand Hill. Roger turned on the headlights and rolled down the window. The temperature dipped even more since he left the bar. The storm was moving in. He turned onto Van Dorn. He was almost home.

Roger took the curve near the farm, fast, needing both lanes to navigate it, as the tires fought to retain their grip on the road. The rain-slickened road had prevented it from doing so, and the truck fishtailed coming out of it. By steering into the skid, he was expertly able to correct it and prevent the pick-up from sliding off the road. The tires squealed and his heart was pounding, but he was able to avoid an accident. The rain started coming down a little harder, but at least, he had made it home before the worst of it.

As soon as he saw it—that big, beautiful, behemoth his father had built, Rogers' eyes lit up, as had the sky around him. Something clicked, inside. A sinister smirk came to his face. It widened.

174

His worries were over. He knew exactly what he had to do.

As Roger was slowing down to pull into the driveway leading to the barn, a blinding flash filled his vision, followed by an ear-piercing explosion. It was so loud that it caused them to ring. The oxygen seemed to, momentarily, be removed from the air. Instinctively, Roger applied the brakes and closed his eyes. He didn't know if he was still on the road, or not, when the truck finally slowed to a stop and stalled. At least the anti-lock braking system had prevented it from skidding.

It seemed longer, but only a few seconds had passed before Roger was able to open his eyes again. He was in time to witness the top third of a large oak tree, lining the property, disintegrate, sending a huge bough crashing into the telephone wires. The cables were struck, squarely and with such force, that they fell to the pavement below. Gigantic sparks flew thirty feet into the air, as the transformer attached to the nearest pole exploded. It looked as if a great fireworks display had gone wrong. The floodlight on the barn flickered brightly with the power surge and blew out, sending glass flying in every direction.

Roger thought it the most spectacular sight he had ever witnessed. He never saw a more beautiful or more destructive display of force. It nearly made him forget why he had been flying home in the first place — almost.

Roger restarted the engine and turned into the driveway leading to the barn. He pulled into the open dock section where, in a few weeks, trucks would be loading up to take his freshly crated potatoes to market. He threw the truck into park before it came to a complete stop and the pick-up rocked violently to a halt. Roger jumped down from the truck and climbed the six steps leading to the main portion of the barn. He reached the door just before the rain started to pick up. Thinking that the storm could be just the cover he needed to complete his gruesome task, Roger grinned. All may not be lost, after all, he thought.

Sweating, as much from the stress as from the heat, Roger ran past the forklifts parked near a wall of empty crates, and headed toward the shipping office. Besides the files, inspection sheets, employee information, and bills of lading stored there, Roger always kept a loaded .357 Colt Python in the top drawer of his desk. He had originally kept it there in case an unruly buyer or truck driver started something, he knew, the old six shooter could finish. As he fumbled in his pockets for the keys in his hip pocket, Roger was smiling, thinking about the time he had had to use it.

.   .   .

Owner-operator Nelson Turner, out of Batavia, pulled up to the loading dock with his new Ford 9000 cab-over, complete with matching forty-foot flatbed. It was truly a sharp rig. At just under 4000 miles, she wasn't even broken in yet. The custom paint job on the side doors, stating Turner Trucking Inc., barely

176

had enough time to dry.

Nelson was a tall, heavyset, middle-aged man with a big barrel chest and equally big smile. He wouldn't go anywhere without his trademark brown, 'Indiana Jones' fedora and oversized belt buckle; each inscribed with the letter 'T'. He had long, cocoa brown hair that he always kept in a neat ponytail. He may have had long hair and a ponytail, but this man was far from feminine. He had massive biceps and thick, muscular legs.

Nelson sat in the cab, drinking his morning coffee out of an old beat-up thermos and reading a newspaper, waiting for his truck to get loaded. Berny Ramirez, the forklift operator, had just gone on break himself, so Roger got on the old '85 and headed for a row of crates. The smell of propane filled the stale dock air. It may have been over 15 years old, but she was still faster than the newer electric Panther he owned.

Roger came back with two crates; one stacked on top of the other, and drove them onto the flatbed. He knew that he should have been loading each crate, separately, being that he wasn't as experienced as Berny, but he had another rig waiting and was hoping to save time. In his haste, however, Roger had left several inches of the forks sticking out from the end of the crates, not realizing it, and rammed the back of Nelson's trailer with them. The unmistakable sound of cracking wood, as the forks went through a board in the front of the trailer was heard by all in the area, but Roger pretended that nothing had happened and went back to get a couple more crates.

The loud, braking noise of splintered wood sent a moderately perturbed Nelson Turner out of the cab to inspect the damage. He was waiting on the dock for Roger when he returned with two more crates. Nelson flagged him down telling him to be more careful, stating that he had just purchased the rig and didn't want anything else to happen to it. He was stern, but not disrespectful or threatening in any way, knowing that the board could have, relatively easily, been replaced. However, Roger had blown it out of proportion. Once again, Rogers' temper got the best of him.

It wasn't that the statement made by the mild-mannered trucker was harsh: after all, it was his truck that Roger had damaged. Roger assumed that the guy was making fun of his driving ability. That was not the case. Nelson just wanted to get his load and move on preferably without any further damage. He had only been trying to stress that point. Being as big as he was, he usually only had to say things once, and then, only in a civil manner.

Roger climbed down from the forklift, taking the key with him, and headed for the shipping office. He intended to make the guy wait until Berny finished with his break. Of course, he never made it clear to the big guy, prompting Nelson to follow him.

"All I want is to finish getting this load, so I can get the hell outa here."

"I didn't tell you, you could come down to my office," Roger said, as he opened the door.

Nelson attempted a different approach. "Look, I'm sorry that I got a little upset, back there. It's my new rig and I don't want anything to happen to it. I can't afford any down time, right now."

"I don't care about your damned problems. Get out of my office, mister. He stated, sitting down behind his desk.

"It's Nelson, Nelson Turner," he said, holding out a big, beefy hand.

"Well Nelly, I asked you, now I'm telling you, to get out of my office."

The sarcasm hit a nerve, but Nelson held himself in check. He had arms of steel and could, easily, have bent Roger in two, packed him into a small crate and, putting the proper postage on him, sent him off to some place above the Arctic Circle where he could cool off. Instead, he took a step closer and began, "Look, can't we be re-"

Roger, believing he was being threatened by the man's advance, pulled out a pistol from the top desk drawer. "And I told YOU to get out."

Nelson held up his hands, as if he were a bank robber who

had just been apprehended and said, "Whoa... Now y-you don't want to do that." He took a tentative step backward. His mouth went dry.

"That's right. Keep goin'," Roger said, waving the gun in the direction of the door.

Nelson sidestepped to the left, not taking his eyes off of the weapon, still holding his hands up. Once he was clear, he turned and ran for the safety of his truck. Not much had ever scared this gargantuan of a man, but that pistol sure did.

Nelson took the six steps on the dock in two bounds and hit the ground running. Stress and adrenalin can make even the biggest man run like an Olympic champion. He threw open the cab door, climbed up inside, and started the engine. Without removing the chocks from under the wheels or checking his side mirrors, Nelson slammed the clutch into the first of the ten gears, and sped off as fast as his rig would go. Under those circumstances, Nelson hadn't even bothered waiting for the two crates to come back off.

The coward that he was, even though he was the one packing a weapon, Roger hadn't come out of the office until he had heard Turner's truck pull away. Berny, just coming back from his break, looked at his boss and said, "Where's he goin'? I haven't even started loading him, yet."

． ． ．

Reaching inside the top drawer of his office desk, Roger pulled out the sharp looking six-inch barrel Colt Python. He tossed it in his hand a couple of times to reacquaint himself with the weight of it. Roger had always liked the way the cold steel felt in his hand. He checked the chambers to see exactly how many bullets were still in it and closed it back up. Four out of the six had a round in it; plenty enough to suit his purpose. Roger grinned. "Let's finish this, shall we," he said, looking down at his piece.

Roger tucked the pistol in the front of his pants and walked, briskly, out from behind the desk. He was on a mission. He wanted to get this over with while the storm was at its peak. He was hoping that the wind would muffle the sound of gunshots. It was quiet out in the country and one could hear a gunshot for miles, except on days like this.

Leaving the office without bothering to shut the door, Roger sprinted down the center aisle, toward the exit. The wind was howling and he could see the rain coming down in sheets. He didn't relish having to leave the safety of the barn in that kind of weather, but he had no choice.

Roger went out into the raging downpour and shut the door behind him. He didn't want the barn to be flooded upon his return. It was coming down hard; like nothing he had ever seen.

The wind was whipping, making the going tougher as he ran for the house. The frequent lightning flashes had given definition to the eerie cloud cover. When he reached the edge of the road, the rain ceased. It was the weirdest thing—pouring one second and not a drop the next. It was as if someone had control of the huge atmospheric faucet and turned it to the 'off' position. Roger slowed his pace. He was soaked.

The reprieve didn't last long. The rain was followed, a few seconds later, by nickel sized hail. Roger could hear the pinging as they bombarded the roof of the barn just before the storm carried them in his direction. What was going on, he thought. Suddenly, they were upon him. The hard beads pummeled his body, stinging the exposed areas of his face and hands. Roger brought his arms up to shield himself when something caught his eye. It was Marty. She was standing at the front door, waving her arm, frantically. Even at that distance, he could see the look of horror on her face. When she saw him look up at her, Marty stopped waving her arm and started pointing at something above his head. "What the hell is she pointing at?" he thought. The hail ceased. Damnedest thing: the ground looked as if winter had arrived about four months early. Roger looked up and saw nothing but clouds speeding past. The woman is cracked. Maybe those blows to the head have caused some kind of traumatic brain injury, he thought. All the more reason to finish her off. Then, he heard it. It wasn't above him, but behind him. Roger turned to face it and froze.

Chapter XII

Vengeance Is Mine...

Marty wondered why Roger had gone into the barn. Maybe, he had decided to wait out the storm in the dry comfort of his office. She wasn't about to take any chances, however, keeping a good eye on the entrance door, at all times.

The rain started coming down in buckets and the wind had picked up considerably, swirling madly in different directions. Lightning flashes had become so frequent, she couldn't tell one from the next. The whole sky was lit up. It was both fascinating and frightening at the same time. She couldn't take her eyes away. Trees were bent over at unnatural angles and creaking from the stress. The wind stripped limbs and branches from the trees and sent them tumbling across the yard. The storm was going to leave a huge mess.

Then, she saw it coming about a half mile away through the field behind the barn. She had never seen one before; only pictures of them on TV and in science magazines, but it was unmistakable. A tornado! It was about a half mile away, cutting a path nearly twenty-five feet across through the potato field. It wasn't a large or, particularly defined funnel cloud, but to Marty, it looked huge. And it was heading straight for the barn. "Oh my God: Roger!"

Looking back at the barn, Marty could see him coming down the dock steps. From that angle, he would not be able to see it. She had to warn him that it was coming, somehow. After all he had done to her—the head games, the lies, and the beatings–she felt that he still didn't deserve to die.

Instinct took over and her reaction was quick. Marty placed her 'good' foot on the floor and reached for her crutch. With every ounce of energy she had left, she pushed herself off of the chair, to a standing position. A searing pain burned its way across her chest, but there was no time to even cry. Marty hopped to the door using the crutch for leverage and, in her haste, stumbled, and nearly fell over. She regained her balance unlocked the door and flung it open. The wind ripped it out of her hand and smashed it into the wall, leaving a round dent from where the doorknob struck it. The rain poured in, soaking her from the waist down.

Roger was running toward the house, his stride hampered by the swirling winds. He was nearly to the road when the rain ceased. She watched as he slowed his pace. Then, it started to hail. Large chunks of ice started pelting everything in their path, including Roger. Marty waved her arm back and forth, trying to get his attention as he tried to shield his face with his arms. It worked. She saw him raise his head to look at her. She pointed at the tornado, (which had become more defined and had cut the distance to the house in half.) The hail stopped, leaving the ground a magnificent white. She watched, in horror, as Roger

184

turned to face the oncoming menace. Why wasn't he moving? It started raining, again. "Get out of there, Roger!"

Marty could feel the weight and dampness of the water on her legs. Her jeans were soaked, but she didn't care. Marty wanted to look away from the scene playing out in front of her, but she could not take her good eye off of Roger. She wondered how he could even remain standing. The wind was so strong she had to keep a tight grip on the doorframe to stay upright.

Roger finally moved, but not the way she had hoped. She watched as he fumbled for something in his pants. He had his back turned to her, so she could not see what it was. He held it briefly at his side. It looked like a gun. Yes, she was sure it was a gun. Marty slowly sank to the floor, realizing that Roger had meant it for her. Stephanie had been right, all along. She could not believe it. "He is actually going to kill me," she whispered. She could feel the remaining strength drain from her body, in defeat.

Marty could hear him yell something at the tornado, but couldn't make it out above the howling of the wind. Then, he raised the weapon, aiming it at the ominous destroyer and fired two shots at it. That, she could hear, but barely. The twister gained ground, moving to within a hundred yards and was closing fast. She sat there and prayed that the end would be quick; for the both of them.

. . .

Roger had never seen a tornado, before this, and he sure didn't want to see this one. They were relatively rare for upstate New York, but not unheard of. It sounded like a fast moving train approaching and at first he could not move. He wanted to run, but the shock of seeing something this menacing, this dangerous, seemed to fix his feet to the pavement beneath him. He could only stare at the monstrosity in total amazement and horror. But, the longer he stood watching its erratic movement destroying his livelihood as it danced across the field, the angrier he became. Roger was viewing his economic demise, one plant at a time.

A small rock whipped past him, grazing his cheek while a larger one flew into the barn, smashing a window. This sent shrapnel flying everywhere. One fragment, carried by the wind, ripped through Rogers' left arm, but since it had been traveling at such a great velocity he had never felt it. He could only see and feel the blood running down his forearm. That finally sent him over the edge. He hurriedly, took the pistol from his jeans and held it at his side. "We don't get those, here! Go Back to HELL where you came from!" he yelled. In defiance, Roger raised the weapon and fired two rounds into it, as if that was, somehow, going to kill it; stop it in its tracks. He closed his eyes and waited for the end.

But, miraculously, that is exactly what had happened. The swirling funnel cloud started breaking up and totally disappeared only a hundred feet away form him. He was only seconds away from being flung to oblivion when it had disappeared. In a moment, it was gone. The roar of the wind suddenly ceased and Roger opened his eyes. Nothing: only a crooked, bare path leading through the rows of potatoes up to him.

Roger looked up to see the remnants of the funnel cloud directly overhead. A primitive, guttural noise belched out of him as he hollered, in victory. He raised his arms above his head, in triumph and pumped his fist in the air. Then, remembering the gun in his hand, Roger looked at the Python. "Two bullets left. Let's end this, shall we."

The wind was still whipping when he turned to head back toward the house. Something new filled his field of vision. In the excitement of the moment, Roger had not realized that he was standing in the middle of the road. He had directed his entire focus to the oncoming tornado and did not see it coming until it was too late. Roger would normally have heard it accelerating from around the curve, but for the howling of the wind. For the second time in as many minutes, Roger Van Dorn froze.

.   .   .

Olivia Suhr was a bright, vivacious, seventeen year old high school student, with an equally bright future ahead of her. She was an honor student as well as the star of both the ladies basketball and volleyball teams. Several colleges were looking to recruit her, based on her amazing talents. Heading into her senior year, Olivia was having the time of her life.

Olivia was driving home from her baby-sitting job at the Randalls. The storm had started to pick up when she left their home. Mrs. Randall had asked her if she had wanted to stay and wait it out, there, telling her that she was welcomed to stay. After giving it some thought, she opted not to. Olivia did not want to seem rude, but Bobby and Donald had given her a run for her money and she had had enough of the boys, for one day.

Partly because she liked the song and knew the lyrics and partly because she wanted to drown out the thunder, Olivia had the radio blasting in her parents Chrysler 300. Lightning lit up the sky around her: but she had never been afraid of thunderstorms-- until that day. The wind was gusting and the rain was coming down in sheets. But, even with the wipers on high, she was having trouble seeing the road. The inexperienced young woman was having a hard time keeping the large vehicle on the pavement, because of it. Knowing the dreadful effects of hydroplaning, from the accident that her cousin had earlier in the summer, Olivia slowed way down. The rain ceased. Then, it started to hail.

As she rounded the 90-degree curve on Van Dorn road, the hail stopped. She had never seen hail as big as that. The ground was covered with millions of round white beads of ice, even though it lasted only a few minutes. She could see small dents in the hood of the car; she knew her parents weren't going to be happy, but there was nothing she could have done differently. As she worried about what her parents were going to say, Olivia saw it.

She couldn't take her eyes off of it. The lower part of it was obscured by the barn, but she saw enough of it to know what it was: a tornado. She could see that it was heading directly for the road; directly in her path. Olivia was terrified. She meant to apply the brake, but in her panic, pushed the accelerator, instead. "Oh God, don't let me die," she screamed.

Suddenly, the tornado disappeared. It had vanished into thin air. She was on a collision course with it and it just dissipated before her eyes. Turning her attention to the road in front of her, Olivia stopped screaming and realized that she was still accelerating. She looked down at the speedometer: 73. The young woman took her foot off the gas pedal and looked back at the road.

Olivia saw the man standing in the middle of the road, but had little time to react. She closed her eyes and slammed on the brake but it was much too late.

.   .   .

Roger didn't have much reaction time, either; less than two seconds. He didn't even have time to close his eyes, once his brain processed the information of what he was seeing. If he only had just a few more seconds, he possibly could have jumped out

189

of the way. But, he was in shock and could not move a muscle. What would have been the point, anyway? The car was upon him. Mercifully, Roger wouldn't have long to wait before impact.

Briefly, Roger heard the sound of brakes engaging and the skidding of the tires. Even though the car was equipped with anti-lock brakes, they were ineffective. Hailstones were everywhere. Trying to stop something as big as this, going seventy miles an hour, on a dry road was difficult, at best. But, this was like trying to stop on a million marbles. Impossible.

Roger could hear the crunching of bone and metal, as well as the young girls screams from inside of the vehicle as the front end of the big Chrysler smashed his legs. Then, pain. Like nothing he had ever felt in all of his 34 years on this planet. Lucky for him it would all be over, soon.

Rogers' right leg was severed at the point of impact, the hood of the 300 slicing neatly through his thigh. The police would later find it in the field about 30 feet from the impact site. It would still have the boot attached. Although crushed, the other leg remained with him as he went airborne for a split second. Already in a semi-unconscious state, his brain frantically tried to shut out the horror of what had been happening. His left shoulder connected with the top of the windshield, several inches below the roofline. Glass shattered, showering Olivia with tiny shards. None got in her eyes: they were tightly closed. Rogers' eyes rolled back in his head as every bone in his shoulder disintegrated.

190

The last sound that Roger heard was the tearing of his arm as it, too, was ripped from the rest of his body. Fortunately for him, he never realized what that sound was.

Roger was down to less than three-quarters of his original self. Blood from the severed arteries spurted, leaving gruesome, bright red stripes down the center of the oyster shell colored roof. What was left of him, bounced once off the trunk and landed in the road. After all that, Roger had never let go his beautiful pistol. It was still clenched, tightly, in his remaining hand. A few jerking motions and a couple of labored breaths and it was over.

.   .   .

Marty, upon seeing the gore of what had happened, reached for her crutch and, once again, used it as leverage to assist her with standing. She had become oblivious to the pain. Her whole body had become numb, as her brain, had also tried shutting out the trauma her body had gone through. As she pulled herself up, Marty saw stars and nearly fell to the ground. Instinct took over. She began to hop on one foot to get the blood flowing and managed to remain upright. She was exhausted.

Continuing to lean on the crutch, Marty was able to hobble down the walkway, being careful not to slip on the hail covered ground. The wind was still strong and nearly knocked her over, but she managed to press on. She was able to get as far as the edge of the driveway before collapsing in a heap at the side of the road. Marty could see the young girl leaning out of the drivers' side, with the door open, emptying the contents of her stomach. The front end of her car finally came to rest after taking a nosedive into the ditch, about a tenth of a mile up the road. Steam was coming out of the ruptured radiator, but the engine was still sputtering. Upon closer examination of the surroundings, Marty could see why the electricity went out. Wires were lying on the road only about fifty yards ahead of where the Chrysler came to rest, along with a good portion of the tree. It was more than evident that it had been struck by lightning.

Marty watched the whole event unfold. She knew that there was nothing the woman could have done to prevent the accident and felt sorry for her. It hadn't been her fault, but she understood that the driver was going to have to live with this moment the rest of her life. She wanted to comfort the girl, to tell her that she had saved her life, but she could honestly go no further.

Marty looked across the road at what remained of her husband, then, lowered her head onto the soft, foam armrest of the crutch. He was a bloody mess, but thankfully, she wasn't able to see his face. Yet, even after all that had happened to Roger, she noticed he still had the revolver in his hand. He still had a tight grip on it.

In disbelief, Marty stared at the weapon, not knowing

192

how she should feel. She didn't think she should feel the way she did. She felt relieved. The rain started to let up and the wind died down considerably. She could feel herself slipping out of consciousness and tried to hang on. It was futile. The sky started to lighten and she felt her eye closing. She felt as if her life was ebbing from her body. She was at peace with that. The last thing she could remember before darkness closed in was the sound of sirens in the distance.

Chapter XIII

Recovery Room

Even before she was able to open her eye, Marty knew she was in a hospital. The constant beeping of the various monitors, along with the nursing staff talking among themselves about her condition had made that quite evident. Slowly, she started to drift back into consciousness. She was alive.

Several minutes later, Marty was able to open her eye. She still didn't have vision in her left one; making her wonder if she had lost sight in it. She could feel a patch over it. She had a slight headache and was a bit groggy, more than likely from the pain medication the doctor had prescribed for her. Marty scanned her surroundings and took a visual inventory of what had been done to her. She noticed the I.V. immediately. The tubing was sticking out of her hand, leading up to a small, sterile bag of solution hanging upside down from a pole. She guessed it was probably a saline and antibiotic drip. She reached under the sheet, and could feel the top of the cast that they had put on her right leg. She hadn't lost that, either.

Marty wondered what time it was and, for that matter, the date. She had no idea just how long she had been under. Looking at the clock on the wall near the entrance, she could see that it was seven minutes to ten and from the way the sunlight was coming in from the window, it had to be morning. Forgetting that she had broken ribs, Marty tried to pull the sheet down, using both hands. The pain wasn't quite as bad as she remembered, but she still moaned in discomfort. She lowered her left arm and continued using only her right. As she figured, she was wearing one of those idiotic blue hospital gowns that didn't cover nearly enough of the human anatomy, especially in the back.

She lifted the gown and noticed a small bandage on the left side of her abdomen. That meant that she had had surgery. She wondered what had been done.

Paula Reinhardt was a short, moderately overweight, black woman in her mid forties. But, because she had taken such good care of her cocoa brown skin, she looked much younger. Paula spent the last 18 years taking care of others, whether at home or at work, which rarely left any time to take care of her own health. More than that, Paula was a phenomenal cook and loved to eat whatever her nimble fingers whipped up. Whenever staff or management threw a party on the unit, Paula had always been the one to whom they came, knowing that she would put her culinary skill to work. They were never disappointed.

Upon hearing the moan, Nurse Paula came into the room, looking down at Marty with compassionate brown eyes. "How are we feeling, today?"

Marty had always hated hearing a nurse say 'we.' She

196

always felt like saying, "I don't know about you, but I sure as hell don't feel good." Instead, because the woman had entered with obvious concern and was only doing her job, Marty placed her right hand on her forehead. "My head hurts and I feel tired and dizzy."

"I can see about getting you some Tylenol. You're not allergic to it, are you?"

"No."

"The dizziness is probably caused by the morphine drip. I can see about turning it down, slightly, if you want. It's just that we felt you have been experiencing significant pain. You were moaning in your sleep."

"That would be great. I have a high tolerance for pain," Marty stated, remembering the events of the last few hours she had been awake. "I don't want to become addicted to it."

"There wouldn't be any chance of you becoming addicted to it. Not for the amount of time you are going to be on it. It isn't long term; just 'til you start healing. It helps you to relax so you can get some rest, but we can still slow it down for you."

"Yes, please. By the way, which hospital am I in and how long have I been out of it?"

"You're at Strong Memorial and you have been here

about 16 hours. It's about ten a.m. You were admitted just after six p.m.," Paula said, matter-of-factly. "You are very popular," she added. "There are several people who want to speak with you."

"Who's that?"

"You're friend, Stephanie is here and Dr. DiLoreto needs to talk to you, oh, and the police officer, outside, needs to speak with you."

"The Police!" She sounded surprised, but quickly realized that an investigator would want to have a word with her. "I guess I should have figured that they might want to ask me some questions. When does he want to talk to me?"

"As soon as the Dr. has been in to see you. That takes precedence. I'll let him know you are awake. He should be in to see you, shortly. He's a top notch ophthalmologist."

"So, I need surgery on my eye. Am I going to be blind?" Marty was worried about her condition.

"I, honestly, cannot answer that question, even if I know the answer, but feel free to ask the doctor anything. He is very personable. You will like him. He has a wonderful personality and a good sense of humor," Paula said with a wink. "Can I get you anything else, before I get the doctor?"

"No. I guess I am all set, but can you at least tell me about the bandage on my stomach? Did I have surgery?"

"Yes. They had to take out your spleen. It was ruptured. The surgery was successful, but I can't tell you anything about your present condition."

Marty looked dejected. She managed a weak "okay."

"I'll check and see about getting you that Tylenol and tell the doctor you're awake."

Marty was worried about her eye. She still couldn't see anything out of it because of the swelling, but knowing that it had only been one day after the events she could remember, put her at ease, somewhat. Still, she hoped that the swelling would have gone down enough for her to see something, at least. Even with a patch on, she believed that she should have been able to see something, if only light and shadows.

Marty tried taking her mind off it by questioning how she had arrived at the hospital in the first place. She hadn't been able to use the phone to call for an ambulance. She remembered that the electricity went out prior to her being able to use it. The young woman in the car that had struck and killed Roger wouldn't have had time to do so, either. The last thing she could remember was hearing sirens coming down the road. Her interest was sparked. How had they been able to get to her so quickly?

As she was still pondering the question, Dr. DiLoreto entered the room. "Hello, Ms. Madeline Van Dorn. I'm David DiLoreto. I'm one of the retina surgeons here at Strong and I wanted to discuss a few things pertaining to your eye and the surgery I'll be performing."

"Am I going to lose my eye, doctor?" she blurted out.

The look of fear was unmistakable.

"I can honestly tell you that you are not going to lose the vision in your left eye," he said with a smile. "But, I do have to go in and repair the damage done to your retina. It is slightly detached, but from what I have seen, it shouldn't be too complicated. Of course, I'll know more once I actually go in."

"Thank God," she said, sighing with relief.

"From what I can see you have been through, you are a lucky woman. It could have been much worse. But, we will let the staff know when we can perform the surgery so they can have you prepped and ready, all right. We will get you in as soon as we can. Try to have a nice morning and get some rest, Ms. Van Dorn."

"You too, doctor and thank you."

"Thank me after the surgery is successful," he said, waving the clipboard with her charts on them.

200

Nurse Paula re-entered the room as soon as the doctor was leaving, saying, "I just wanted to give you the Tylenol you had asked for before the police officer came in to see you. Here you go." She said, handing Marty a little plastic cup with two capsules in it along with a small paper cup of water.

"Thank you, Paula."

"The officer will be in to see you, now, Madeline. I hope everything goes well for you."

"You can call me Marty, if you would like. Everyone calls me Marty."

"Okay, Marty. Good luck."

Marty barely had enough time to catch her breath before the next gentleman came in to see her. He was wearing the familiar New York State Troopers uniform and was very different from Dr. DiLoreto. Nurse Reinhardt had been right. She was becoming very popular, but she sure could have done without this visit. He had been standing just outside the doorway, talking with the nurses, while the doctor discussed her condition with her. His countenance changed immediately, once he entered the room. The hard brimmed troopers' hat was intimidating and she became visibly nervous.

"Mrs. Van Dorn, I'm Trooper Robert Forsythe with the New York State Police. I'd like to ask you a few questions if you are feeling up to it?" That wasn't really a question. She had better be feeling up to it. "I'm heading up the investigation on what took place at your farm, yesterday," he said, sternly.

"I kind of figured that someone was going to want to talk to me," she told him, looking down at her hands. She noticed that she was still wearing her wedding rings on the left.

"And why is that, Mrs. Van Dorn."

"Well, you have to know that I wasn't hit by the car, for one thing."

The trooper had interrogated many suspects in the past 23 years as a police officer. He knew she was going to spill, everything. He just folded his arms across his chest and said nothing. Marty continued "And you probably went into the house and found the rifle in the window."

"Among other things. Would you like to explain why it was in the window and who is was meant for?" Again, not a question. "Your fingerprints were all over it." How quickly he had gone from laughing and joking with the nurses to the stern, seriousness Marty was witnessing at the moment.

Marty told him everything she could remember about the previous day. It was hard to believe that it had been less than 20 hours since her life had completely unraveled. She told him about the beating, splinting her leg, the pain she felt as she made her way downstairs, and the call to Stephanie.

Trooper Forsythe interrogated a visibly shaken Marty Van Dorn for almost 15 minutes. He had conducted many interviews and questioned many suspects in the past and was expert at distinguishing truth from a lie. He couldn't find any holes in her story. "Now, is there anything else you can remember, Mrs. Van Dorn; anything you want to add?"

"No sir, officer." The suspense was killing her and she had to know. "Am I going to jail?"

"Technically, Mrs. Van Dorn, you did have a loaded weapon in your home and, by your own admittance, had it pointed in a threatening manner at your husband. However, I'm going to talk with Stephanie and a couple of people around Rusty's Roost. If your story can be corroborated I don't think, based on what you have told me, the evidence found, and what you have been through, that there would be any charges filed against you." The trooper got up from the chair he had been sitting in. "You have been through enough, already. But, if not, I'll know where to find you. I don't think that you will be leaving here anytime, soon. If you think of anything later on that you believe would help in our investigation, please, let me know. Here is my card," he said, handing it to her.

"Thank you, Trooper Forsythe."

"Try to have a nice day, Mrs. Van Dorn. I hope you recover, soon."

. . .

Another 15 minutes went by when a mildly shaken Stephanie Stafford entered her friends' room. Marty, relieved that it was unlikely that she was going to go to jail, had been dozing. That, along with the morphine drip, had calmed her down, considerably. But it seemed that even after the ordeal was over, it was not completely over.

Stephanie, purposely making noise by pretending to accidentally bump the chair next to her bed, had awakened her. In one hand, she had a bouquet of flowers; in the other, a copy of the morning newspaper. On the front page, in bold 1 1/2 inch, capitol letters, read 'TORNADO HITS MARION.' The caption underneath stated 'One Man Dead As Result.'

Marty looked over at her best friend as Stephanie sat down. "Hi, Steph. I'm so glad you're here. I'm a wreck."

"Why wouldn't I be here for you? You are my best

friend. You look terrible, Marty; even worse than I imagined." She couldn't hide the tears.

"Gee, thanks."

"I'm so sorry. Can you forgive me?" she asked, as she clutched Marty's hand.

"Forgive you. For what, Steph?"

"For calling the police. I waited as long as I could, but I couldn't sit back and let anything else happen to you."

"I wondered how they were able to arrive, so quickly. Believe it or not, those sirens were the last things I can remember hearing before I passed out. I should have known it was you."

"What the heck happened after I talked to you, yesterday? I mean, besides this," Stephanie said, showing her the newspaper and laying it open on the blanket across her legs.

Marty told her everything that happened: from scooting across the floor into her bedroom, to the gruesome accident and her passing out. She stated how Roger had gone into the barn to retrieve the pistol and how he had shot at the tornado with it.

"I told you that he was trying to kill you, Marty."

"I know you did. I'm sorry for doubting you."

"And that is what I just told the state trooper, too."

"You did?"

"Yes I did," Stephanie stated with pride. "I told him what a controlling creep Roger was and that that hadn't been the first time he laid his hands on you, either."

"Thanks, Steph. I'm so sorry that you had to get involved." Marty lowered her head in shame.

"You have nothing to be ashamed of, Marty. You put up with a lot of garbage, trying to make a bad marriage work. You should be commended." Then, as an afterthought, "Why didn't you ever call me or the Victims Resource Center, or even a shelter for battered women? There must be one or two in the area."

"I felt ashamed to admit that there was a problem. Besides, once Roger found out where I was, he might have done something worse to me. If I stayed with you, he could have done something to you or your family. That was something I wouldn't have been able to live with. He thought of me as just another possession and was capable of almost anything when he got that angry. It was best to just leave him alone for a while to let him cool off. Once he calmed down, Roger was back to his normal self."

"You're still in denial. How could he go back to 'normal' when he never was? He was like that for years, Marty, and he wasn't ever going to change."

"Again, you're probably right. I couldn't change his way of thinking, so I should have changed mine. If I knew that it was going to end like this, I might have left a long time ago.

"So, what are your plans, now? Are you going to leave Marion?"

"I haven't thought about it, yet. I haven't had the time to think about it. Everything has happened so quickly. I'm still in shock. I can't believe Roger is dead. I can't believe I am a widow. I can't believe any of this is real."

"I can understand about you not having time to think about it. I can't believe any of this is real, either."

"But," Marty finished, "since you asked me, I can honestly say that I do not want to leave this town, at least, not immediately. It is such a quiet, wonderful place to raise a family and I hope to have children, someday."

"I'm glad you said that. I was afraid you would want to move away and I wouldn't want you to," Stephanie said, giving Marty's hand a gentle shake. Looking into Stephanie's eyes, Marty could see that she was telling the truth. After months of not talking to her, she couldn't believe Stephanie still liked her, much less considered her, her best friend. "I'm very lucky to have a friend like you, Steph."

They hugged, like two sisters who had been adopted by different families and were finally able to be reunited after many years. Stephanie wanted to hold her tighter, but was afraid of hurting her. Marty wouldn't have cared.

"Hey," Stephanie said, holding her away at arms length. "I've got something in my purse that just might cheer you up."

"I don't think much of anything is going to cheer me up, Steph."

"This might," she said, grabbing her purse by one handle and quickly starting to fumble through it. Stephanie took out her checkbook opened it, and pulled out a business card. Handing it to Marty, she said, "Zachary gave this to me at the class reunion. He said that if you or I needed anything to give him a call."

Marty looked at it and snickered.

"What's so funny?"

"This seems so typical of something that Zachary would come up with. It's so plain. He hasn't changed in 15 years."

"That's what I thought when I first saw it."

As much as it hurt to do so, Marty laughed with Stephanie joining in. After a moment of much needed stress relief, the two of them calmed down. Nurse Paula looked in to see if

Marty was all right and, seeing the two of them in mild hysterics, knew that she was fine and had left the room.

Marty looked over at her friend, becoming serious. She had known Stephanie nearly 16 years, to the day. They had been through so much, together; important life issues: weddings, babies and now, this. Marty felt no closer to anyone than she did to Stephanie. "I want to thank you for everything; for coming here and sticking by me, even after all those months we hadn't talked. I'm sorry."

"It's okay, Marty. You would have been there for me. You HAVE been there for me. I wouldn't be the woman I am today without your help."

"That's very nice of you to say," Marty said, holding back another round of tears. Then, holding up Zachary's card, she added, "I want to thank you for this, too, but I don't know if I'm going to call him."

"Why not?"

"Two reasons," Marty sighed. "I realize that, as of yesterday, I am no longer married. It hasn't sunk in, yet. I have a great deal to think about. It's too soon to be thinking about another relationship. There is just something wrong with doing that. I wouldn't want anyone to think I was a tramp. But, not only that, I'm a mess. Look at me. I look ugly, now. No man would want to give me the time of day, much less, date me. Roger never let me go to school. I'm uneducated. No one is going to want me, right now. It's not that I have low self-esteem, I have NO self-esteem. I am nothing."

"Marty, you are a highly intelligent, beautiful woman. You are going to heal from this. It should be much easier for you to go back to school, since you don't have any children to take care of. And I'm not saying that you have to date, right away. But, what is wrong with giving the man a courtesy call, letting him know that you are all right. I'm sure that he read today's paper."

Marty picked up the newspaper and read the main headline. "I guess we're big news, huh."

Stephanie looked at her watch. It was 11:35. "Listen. I have a couple of errands to run. Saturday is the only day I can seem to manage to find the time to do anything. Drake is home cleaning up the yard from the storm and I'm sure he is going to watch Tiger Woods play golf, later, but after that I'm sure he won't mind watching the kids long enough for me to come back up here to see you for a couple of hours."

"That will be great. It will be nice to see you. I'm sure I'll be out of surgery by then. They have to go in and repair a detached retina in my eye."

"It sounds bad."

"The doctor said that it is a relatively easy procedure. He said it shouldn't take long. The important thing is that I won't lose my eye."

"No doubt. I wish you didn't have to go through this, Marty."

"I'll be okay. You just go home to your family. I'm not going anywhere for awhile."

"Alright, but I promise to be back, later." Pointing to Zachary's business card, she added, "Give it some thought, Marty."

"I will," she said, although she didn't have any real intention of doing so.

"You have been given a second chance at life. Don't blow this opportunity."

"I'm grateful for all you have done, Steph. Please, don't be upset with me."

"I could never be upset with you, Marty. I'm upset for you, not with you. I'll see you later. Take care," Stephanie said, giving her a sad puppy-eyed look as she left.

Marty tried to get some sleep, but her thoughts were running rampant. Even with the morphine they had been giving her; she just couldn't become drowsy enough. In spite of telling herself not to think about Zachary, Marty couldn't help doing so. She honestly felt that calling him at this point in time would make her look desperate and trashy. She decided to give it some more thought.

Picking up the newspaper, Marty began to read the article about what had occurred the day before; at least how the staff writer had interpreted it. In this case, the media had most of what happened, wrong, but in all fairness, the writer could not have known all the facts. Because there was an investigation in progress, the police probably did not give the reporter a great deal of information about the incident. The story was printed as a tragic case of a young couple being in the wrong place at the wrong time- just two people trying to outrun a tornado when a car struck them. Nothing, at all, was mentioned about a weapon. But, for Marty, that was a good thing. Without a weapon, no one would question why an arrest had not been made. She was totally exonerated.

Marty tossed the paper into the same chair that Stephanie was sitting in, grappling with the realization that she did have at least one difficult phone call to make. She made a promise, if only to herself. Gingerly, she reached for the phone, sitting on the nightstand and placed it on her thigh. She could hear the annoying monotonous tone as she lifted the receiver off of its base. A tear welled in her eye, blurring her vision. It spilled over and slowly rolled down her cheek. She put the receiver back in its cradle and waited until she had regained her composure.

After a minute or two, Marty was able to resume her call. She wiped her face with the edge of the highly starched sheet, catching the strong scent of bleach. This is ridiculous, she thought. It shouldn't be this damned difficult. Yet, for her, it was. It was one of the most difficult phone calls she ever had to make. But, why? This wasn't some old friend from high school that she hadn't talked to in ten years or a second cousin she only saw at weddings and funerals. This was her mother.

It wasn't the fact that she had thought that her mother was angry and wouldn't want to speak to her, either. Marty knew beyond a doubt that her mother loved her and always would. She was embarrassed and ashamed that she had only called her mother a few times since the year started—the last being on Mother's Day. Her mother had always been there for her and she deserved to be treated better than how Marty had treated her. It was as simple and as complicated as that.

Marty didn't want this next call to be an unpleasant one. She didn't want it to get her mother upset and make her worry. But because of the subject matter and the information she was about to give her, how could her mother not get upset. "Hi, mom. How are you? By the way Roger beat the hell out of me. He broke my leg and ribs and they had to take out my spleen, but don't worry he's dead. He got run over by a car." How could she possibly make the details of what happened sound upbeat and cheerful? Impossible.

The longer she waited, the more difficult it would become.

She picked up the receiver once more and dialed the number from memory. After the second ring, her mother answered the phone. She sounded like she was in the next room. As the tears started to well up in her eyes, once again, Marty said, "Hello, mom. You got a while? We have got a lot to talk about."